Er

MW01612289

"For anyone feeling weary or defeated by the relentless hard knocks of this mortal life, Tim Shorey's *From a High Mountain* is an absolute gift. With the magisterial text of Isaiah 40 as the focal point, this personal, relatable, and deeply comforting devotional fixes our gaze on the God who 'does not grow faint or grow weary,' and invites us to slow down and savor Scripture's comforting, eternal words of life."

Brett McCracken, senior editor, The Gospel Coalition; author, *The Wisdom Pyramid: Feeding Your Soul in a Post-Truth World*

"Part pastoral commentary and part devotional, these meditations on Isaiah 40 explicate the famous chapter in a stirring way. Tim has an ability to nurture an image or word in our imagination in order for its truth to seize us. But he doesn't remain in the biblical world. He also employs his sufferings as a prism to showcase God's mercy and truth as the comfort we all need. This book will bring soul-level blessing into the heart of anyone who reads it."

Jonathan Dodson, founder of Gospel-Centered Discipleship, Theologian in Residence in Citizens' Church, author of several books, including *The Unbelievable Gospel: Say Something Worth Believing* and *Gospel-Centered Discipleship*

"Helpfully personal and deeply pastoral, the reflections Tim offers in this book will help you to behold the God of all comfort when all seems lost. If you're feeling wounded and worn out by life, let this book put words to your discouragement as it braces your heart with glorious, biblical truth."

Christine Chappell, author, *Midnight Mercies: Walking with God through Depression in Motherhood*; host, Hope + Help Podcast; certified biblical counselor

"These meditations are so good! Tim pastors well through them, with a style that fairly crackles at times—a hard thing to pull off stylistically in devotionals without sounding forced. But these musings don't sound forced; they sound like Tim. It's not easy to share personal sufferings as Tim has done, but in doing so, he has made himself a parable, not a focus. The real star of this wonderful and pastorally sensitive journey through Isaiah 40 is our merciful Lord Jesus, the one who suffered like no other has, all to God's glory. Tim is relentless in truthing his trials with God's promises, shoring us up against the despair of pain in a fallen world."

Scott Faris, pastor, Sovereign Grace Church, Marlton, NJ

"This book is a rare jewel with immense power to enlighten and comfort the people of God. Written in a wonderfully descriptive and illuminating style, Tim masterfully exposits the word of God and provides a rich exposition of Isaiah 40 without a hint of cold intellectualism. The whole book is beautifully personal and aimed right at the heart, thereby sharing with us the comfort with which he has been comforted. What a resource for weary sufferers in need of the God who comforts!"

Conor Anderson, past professor of Philosophy, Theology, and Biblical Studies at the University of San Diego and San Diego Christian College; current pastor of Penngrove Community Church in Northern California

"Tim's reflections out of Isaiah 40 on the character and comfort of God are foundational, life-sustaining truths. This devotional is a transforming perspective providing genuine hope for everyone to embrace. I recommend this resource for every pastor and counselor who is helping others to know and experience God in the uncertainties of life."

Joe Carnuccio, Executive Director/Counselor, God Changes Lives Ministries, Inc.

"The first time I heard Tim Shorey preach, his sermon text was Isaiah 40. It was a feast. Tim has spent decades mining this great chapter, and I am thrilled that he is now sharing those insights in print. This is a powerful little book. Our God, who is the God of all comfort, has comforted Tim in his afflictions so that he is able to comfort those who are in any affliction. These God-centered reflections from Isaiah 40 have strengthened my soul, and they will strengthen yours also."

Jared Mellinger, Senior Pastor, Covenant Fellowship Church, Glen Mills, PA, and author of *A Bright Tomorrow: How to Face Your Future without Fear* and *Think Again: Relief from the Burden of Introspection*

"Tim Shorey is my friend. We have served side by side in pastoral ministry and have shared the joy and adventure of planting a church together. But Tim has carried burdens I know not of. As we have walked together over the years his footprints have gone deeper than mine. His pace has slowed, but the fire in his heart and the faith in his soul have never lost their heat or their light. This devotional comes from the inner workings of a life in love with the Savior and rich in theological reflection. There is sorrow here, there is perplexity, there is pain. But there is always hope. I heartily commend it to you if you are in a season of sorrow. Or if you care for people who are living in the heavy shadows of suffering. But maybe most of all, I commend it to every follower of Christ because suffering comes with the journey for all of us."

Andy Farmer, pastor, board member of the Biblical Counseling Coalition, author of *Real Peace: What We Long for and Where to Find It* and *Trapped: Getting Free from People, Patterns, and Problems*

"Maturing disciples of Jesus learn to weave Bible passages into their lives through daily meditations. Tim Shorey has done this in his latest book *From a High Mountain: 31 Reflections on the Character and Comfort of God.* These meditations from Isaac 40 are a gift modeling for us how sacred words intertwine with our daily difficulties. Tim shows us from his own journey through his sufferings with cancer how his gaze on God's glory has sustained him, and then transported him to a high place of hope and confidence. I have found Tim's reflections stirring and strengthening in my own shadowy journey. Whatever your difficult season, I recommend that you read these daily reflections slowly to find powerful comfort as you move forward."

> **David Pinckney,** Regional Director, Acts 29 Church Planting
> Network and Missions Pastor, River of Grace Church, NH

"Isaiah 40 is a treasure-trove of comforting truth, and Tim Shorey digs deep to mine its riches. Whether you are faced with disappointment, disaster, or despair, this devotional will lift your eyes to behold God, reminding you of his absolute sovereignty and unchanging goodness. Life in a broken world is painful. Read this and let each reflection encourage your weary heart."

> **Amy DiMarcangelo,** Equipped for Mercy resources, and
> author of *Go and Do Likewise: A Call to Follow Jesus in a
> Life of Mercy* and *A Hunger for More: Finding Satisfaction
> in Jesus When the Good Life Doesn't Fill You*

From a High Mountain

FROM A
HIGH
MOUNTAIN

31 Reflections on the Character and Comfort of God

(Based on Isaiah 40)

Timothy M. Shorey

From My Youth

From a High Mountain: 31 Reflections on the Character and Comfort of God

From My Youth
Newark, DE

Cover image: Adobe photos
Cover and interior design: Benjamin Vrbicek
Author photo: Douglas Martin Nottage

Paperback ISBN: 979-8-2185-5140-7
Ebook ISBN: 979-8-2185-5141-4

Contents

*To all those who have faithfully followed
my cancer journal and incessantly stormed
the high heavens in prayer for my healing.
Words are too poor to speak our gratitude.*

– Tim and Gayline

Preface

The title of this book, *From a High Mountain*, is taken from Isaiah 40:9, where God commands his prophet to scale a high mountain to herald the good news and glory of God. But the content of this book was conceived in a very hot furnace.

From our earliest days of married life, Gayline (my wife of 47 years) and I have experienced many deep and prolonged trials. Married young (at 19 and 20), trials soon followed. As a result, we have never known adult life, except in the fire and through tears.

We have had two children barely survive life-threatening conditions. When I was 30 (36 years ago) I contracted a serious meningitis-like virus that damaged the nerve lining in my head, and left me with a permanent 24/7/365 headache, registering high on the pain Richter scale. And what shall I say about my serious lumbar injuries that have resisted treatment, and my advancing arthritis, both of which have added greatly to my daily discomfort.

But these are my minor afflictions. My most recent and serious trials have included a diagnosis of stage 4 incurable cancer with an uncertain prognosis. Soon after that diagnosis I contracted actinomycosis (a rare bone disease nicknamed "lumpy jaw disease" for the damaging effect it can have on the jaw bone). It is an extremely painful bacterial bone infection that so far has resisted twelve months of 24/7 intravenous antibiotic treatments (infused via a PICC-line in my chest, and a pump and ever-present medicinal pack over my shoulder). Doctors assure me that as of this moment, the treatments are not getting the job done, and an extremely painful surgical procedure on my jaw-bone, teeth, and gum, followed by even longer antibiotic treatments, is the only way forward.

Prolonged treatments for both of my diseases have had painfully debilitating side effects on my physical condition and mental well-being. And there is no sign of imminent healing. As might be imagined, all of these sorrows have led to multiplied and ever-accumulating losses (not the least of which was a medically compelled resignation from 40 years of pastoral ministry). I will not recite all my losses here, but will say simply that their effects have radically altered my life in every conceivable way.

Perhaps most difficult of all is that I don't know where any of this is heading, or how long it all will last, or if I will survive. The uncertainty can be emotionally debilitating—were it not for the comfort of God. And it is that comfort that I want to share in this collection of devotional meditations.

Consider this devotional to be me heralding from the "high mountain" of my chair and computer, the everlasting character and comfort of God (Isa. 40:1, 9). In this collection of thirty-one reflections, I affirm with a grateful heart that my many and difficult afflictions have made the God of Isaiah 40 the greatest comfort and Comforter my heart could ever desire.

My hope, my faith, and my joy would never have survived these long ordeals, were it not for the consoling love and character of the One described in Isaiah's prophecy. My gratitude to this God is what has inspired this contribution to the devotional life of the Church. This is my offering of praise to a God who has found me in my need and comforted me all the way.

Still in the grip and grace of God,
Tim

Finding God When All Seems Lost

If you need comfort, you need God. That's the main point of this book.

From a High Mountain began as a cancer journal entry based on Isaiah 40 and became this 31-day devotional volume. This happened because in a recent re-read of Isaiah 40, I was affected by its heralded truth as much as I ever have been; which is saying much, since I have read this chapter countless times for both personal devotion and sermon preparation purposes. To this day it remains, in my experience and view, the most comforting text in all the Bible.

In my recent return to Isaiah 40, I was reminded that its every line impacts the heart with comforting and humbling truth. So I decided to write a real-time day by day, right here, right now, sentence-by-sentence series of journal entries on Isaiah 40, composed as I linger in the shadows of my own present trials. I have felt a deep longing to slow down and reflect on each and every sentence (or question) Isaiah records, and this is the result.

Nothing Shall Be Left

One reason why I love Isaiah 40 is because it's all about God comforting his people (first, the ancient Hebrew people, and now, us) who were beset by all kinds of sorrows, just as I often have been, and am right now. We see into the Israelites' world by looking backwards in the text. Isaiah 39:5–7 provides us with the historical context for Isaiah 40. We read there that the people were about to be exiled from their homeland to distant Babylon.

The outcome of Babylon's invasion and Israel's exile is expressed poignantly with the words that, of all that they possessed, "nothing would be left" (Isa. 39:6). This means that Isaiah 40 proclaims comfort for God's people because Isaiah 39 predicts ruin for them. Isaiah 40 is about experiencing God when ruin happens. It's about finding God when all seems lost.

The events foretold in Isaiah 39 were fulfilled some time later (one account is in 2 Chron. 36:5–21). Following a two-year siege, Nebuchadnezzar, king of Babylon, broke through Israel's defenses to ravage and savage the land. This meant that Israel's world was melting down. Filled with international evil, despotic oppression, and unspeakable sin, nearly every square inch of real estate on planet earth was becoming a landfill of corruption, a war zone of sin and ruin.

That's what exile does. It takes everything. When exile's dust settles, nothing but dust remains. In Israel's case, their violently enforced dispersement into an angry evil world involved the destruction of homes, the pillaging of possessions, the loss of land and jobs, the obliteration of familiar institutions, the ripping up of cultural and traditional roots, the raping of daughters and wives, the rending of families, the relocation of a population, the possible loss of family and national identity, an enslavement of the able-bodied, and an utter loss of freedom—all at the hands of a Hitler-like despot. And God had predicted that there would be no hope of restoration of any of it in the people's lifetime.

This is the *warfare* (or wearisome toil) of which Isaiah 40:2 speaks. The Hebrew word speaks of servitude, hardship, and sorrow in a war zone. Israel was in an unparalleled and appalling season of troubles.

I Have an Inkling

I would never claim sorrows beyond what are real, but I think I do have an inkling of what Israel felt. Not that I would compare my woes with theirs (for that would be neither accurate, nor helpful), but I can relate to their sorrows. And while I cannot say that of *all* that I've possessed, "nothing has been left," I can say that of the *much* that I have possessed, much has been lost.

This is one reason why Isaiah 40 means so much to me. Isaiah 40 is not an abstract treatise about God or an academic term paper about the nature and problem of suffering. It is God's compassionate love expressed to comfort those he loves—people like you and me who are going through the flame and flood (Isa. 43:2) and need to hope against hope that God will land them safely on the other side.

Real Comfort in Real Suffering

Isaiah 40 is real time comfort for real time suffering. And I am glad it is. I have little patience with platitudes. I've seen and felt too much of what is real to resort to what is pat and clichéd.

From a High Mountain has been written in the face of that reality. Always real, and sometimes raw, this devotional journal (for these are in fact excerpts from my cancer journal) will address things as they really are, and apply God's comfort to them. It is my hope that this will comfort others, in part by giving them a sense of freedom to be authentic in their own afflictions, even as I am in mine.

In *From a High Mountain,* I have proclaimed Isaiah's prophecy one sentence at a time, as a 31-day devotional that offers real reflections on the comforting character of the One whom Paul calls "the Father of mercies and God of all comfort." And I am doing so while going through very real sorrows that require that comfort. My hope is that it will provide others with daily comfort, with the same comfort that I have received from God (2 Cor. 1:3–4).

As for this work itself, *From a High Mountain* is a one month daily devotional. It consists of 31 substantial meditations of consistent accessible length. As such, it can supplement other devotional resources for a single month of the reader's life.

Because *From a High Mountain* is essentially an excerpt from my cancer journal, it will include some very personal, sometimes raw content. This preserves the feel of a journal, while providing a devotional, theological, and pastoral verse-by-verse exposition to benefit the heart.

My prayer is that *From a High Mountain* will introduce readers to a passage of Scripture that in the five decades of my faith journey, has never lost its power to comfort me in all our varied seasons and sufferings of life.

Isaiah 40

¹ *Comfort, comfort my people, says your God.*
² *Speak tenderly to Jerusalem,*
*   and cry to her*
that her warfare is ended,
*   that her iniquity is pardoned,*
that she has received from the LORD's hand
*   double for all her sins.*

³ *A voice cries:*
"In the wilderness prepare the way of the LORD;
*   make straight in the desert a highway for our God.*
⁴ *Every valley shall be lifted up,*
*   and every mountain and hill be made low;*
the uneven ground shall become level,
*   and the rough places a plain.*
⁵ *And the glory of the LORD shall be revealed,*
*   and all flesh shall see it together,*
*   for the mouth of the LORD has spoken."*

⁶ *A voice says, "Cry!"*
*   And I said, "What shall I cry?"*

All flesh is grass,
   and all its beauty is like the flower of the field.
⁷ *The grass withers, the flower fades*
   when the breath of the Lᴏʀᴅ blows on it;
   surely the people are grass.
⁸ *The grass withers, the flower fades,*
   but the word of our God will stand forever.

⁹ *Go on up to a high mountain,*
   O Zion, herald of good news
lift up your voice with strength,
   O Jerusalem, herald of good news;
   lift it up, fear not;
say to the cities of Judah,
   "Behold your God!"
¹⁰ *Behold, the Lord Gᴏᴅ comes with might,*
   and his arm rules for him;
behold, his reward is with him,
   and his recompense before him.
¹¹ *He will tend his flock like a shepherd;*
   he will gather the lambs in his arms;
he will carry them in his bosom,
   and gently lead those that are with young.

¹² *Who has measured the waters in the hollow of his hand*
   and marked off the heavens with a span,
enclosed the dust of the earth in a measure
   and weighed the mountains in scales
   and the hills in a balance?
¹³ *Who has measured the Spirit of the Lᴏʀᴅ,*

or what man shows him his counsel?
¹⁴ Whom did he consult,
   and who made him understand?
Who taught him the path of justice,
   and taught him knowledge,
   and showed him the way of understanding?
¹⁵ Behold, the nations are like a drop from a bucket,
   and are accounted as the dust on the scales;
   behold, he takes up the coastlands like fine dust.
¹⁶ Lebanon would not suffice for fuel,
   nor are its beasts enough for a burnt offering.
¹⁷ All the nations are as nothing before him,
   they are accounted by him as less than nothing and emp-
      tiness.

¹⁸ To whom then will you liken God,
   or what likeness compare with him?
¹⁹ An idol! A craftsman casts it,
   and a goldsmith overlays it with gold
   and casts for it silver chains.
²⁰ He who is too impoverished for an offering
   chooses wood that will not rot;
he seeks out a skillful craftsman
   to set up an idol that will not move.
²¹ Do you not know? Do you not hear?
   Has it not been told you from the beginning?
   Have you not understood from the foundations of the
      earth?

²² It is he who sits above the circle of the earth,
*   and its inhabitants are like grasshoppers;*
who stretches out the heavens like a curtain,
*   and spreads them like a tent to dwell in;*
²³ who brings princes to nothing,
*   and makes the rulers of the earth as emptiness.*

²⁴ Scarcely are they planted, scarcely sown,
*   scarcely has their stem taken root in the earth,*
when he blows on them, and they wither,
*   and the tempest carries them off like stubble.*

²⁵ To whom then will you compare me,
*   that I should be like him? says the Holy One.*
²⁶ Lift up your eyes on high and see:
*   who created these?*
He who brings out their host by number,
*   calling them all by name;*
by the greatness of his might
*   and because he is strong in power,*
*   not one is missing.*

²⁷ Why do you say, O Jacob,
*   and speak, O Israel,*
"My way is hidden from the LORD,
*   and my right is disregarded by my God"?*
²⁸ Have you not known? Have you not heard?
The LORD is the everlasting God,
*   the Creator of the ends of the earth.*
He does not faint or grow weary;

his understanding is unsearchable.
[29] *He gives power to the faint,*
  and to him who has no might he increases strength.
[30] *Even youths shall faint and be weary,*
  and young men shall fall exhausted;
[31] *but they who wait for the LORD shall renew their*
    strength;
  they shall mount up with wings like eagles;
they shall run and not be weary;
  they shall walk and not faint.

Comfort My People

Comfort, comfort my people, says your God.

Isaiah 40:1

Isaiah 40 opens with one sentence, seven words, five truths, and innumerable joys.

Here are the truths which God brings to my mind:

1. *We need comfort.* This verse wouldn't be here if life was a breezy cruise on a well-appointed yacht. God speaks his comfort because we need it. Look at the world and look in the mirror. So much of life is stormy grey.

When my head was still waking up on the pillow this morning my body was already wearied with affliction. My head ached, my teeth and jaw hurt, my back was stiff and weak, I coughed my incessant cough, my legs hurt to stand, I knew I still had cancer and a bone disease and my heart felt heavy because that's what every morning has been like and will be like until God makes me new.

I've got my list, and you've got yours. O, how I (we) need comfort!

2. God is a comforter. I notice that *God* is the one who says, "Comfort my people." *God* says it! The Hebrew word for God is "Elohim." It's the word used in Genesis 1:1, "In the beginning God created the heavens and the earth." He is Elohim, the Almighty Creator-Ruler who is all-wise, all-good, all-holy and just, and everywhere-present throughout all space, time, and eternity. And *that* God cares enough about me in all my pathetic weakness (and about all of us) to say repeatedly, "Comfort my people." What a wonder this is! God Almighty doesn't ignore or scold my tears; he feels and consoles them.

3. God comforts earnestly. God says, "Comfort, comfort my people." Then immediately, he adds, "Speak tenderly to Jerusalem . . ." That's three comfort-imperatives in a sentence and a half. Comfort. Comfort. Speak tenderly. Can you feel God's earnest care and concern? I can. Such repetition means that God is tenderly earnest and emphatic in his comfort. Seeing his children suffer, he yearns for us to be comforted.

4. God comforts personally. I love the personal possessive pronouns God uses. He calls us "my" people and assures us that he is our (your) God. These words suggest affectionate relationship and belonging. God is near and dear to us, and we to him. Are we hurting? We belong to God. Are we ill and dying? We belong to God. Are we abandoned and afraid? We belong to God. Are we afflicted with cancer or some other disease? We belong to God. Do we feel lost, lonely, and left behind? We belong to God. We are his and he is ours. It really is about relationship . . . with *God.*

5. God comforts covenantally. God uses "my people/your God" words to indicate that he doesn't just comfort us personally; he comforts us *covenantally*.

These "possession" claims are common biblical-covenantal language—not unlike a wedding vow—between God and all those who pledge their faith, obedience, and devotion to him. Jeremiah expands like this:

> Now therefore thus says the LORD, the God of Israel [and of all who believe in Jesus] . . . 'I will . . . make them dwell in safety. And they shall be my people, and I will be their God. I will give them one heart and one way, that they may fear me forever . . . I will make with them an everlasting covenant, that I will not turn away from doing good to them . . . I will rejoice in doing them good, and I will plant them in this land in faithfulness, with all my heart and all my soul. (Jer. 32:36–41; brackets added)

So when God invokes this "my people/your God" language in Isaiah 40:1, he is reassuring us that his comforting love is part of his covenant promise to us, and he is welcoming us as his own people, in filial love. We are his covenant people whom he has chosen, whom Jesus ransomed and redeemed on the cross, and whom the Holy Spirit indwells and empowers for life. Behold how God loves his people and seeks their comfort with covenantal and steadfast love!

Isaiah 40 is more than a record of God's comfort in the past. It is God's inviolable covenant reminder of his comfort for all his people in every place, throughout all of time and eternity. Having pledged to be our God and to choose, include, and adopt us as his own treasured people, he is pouring out his comfort on those he loves.

All of that in one seven-word sentence!

Hallelujah!

Speak Tenderly to Jerusalem

Speak tenderly to Jerusalem,
* and cry to her*
that her warfare is ended,
* that her iniquity is pardoned,*
that she has received from the LORD's hand
* double for all her sins.*

Isaiah 40:2

We have already seen in verse 1 of Isaiah 40 that God tells Isaiah twice to comfort his exiled and afflicted people. And then adds quickly in verse 2, "speak tenderly to Jerusalem." The Hebrew means "speak to the heart" of Jerusalem. This is the tender heart of our God; the God who yearns for his comfort to reach down into our depths.

He is saying, "Isaiah, comfort; please comfort my people. And aim for their hearts o man of God, because that is where they are broken, hurting, guilty, ashamed, and afraid. Cry—or cry aloud—to her that there is mercy and pardon with me!"

Three Comfort Promises

My life is marked by a litany of sorrows, fears, and uncertainties. Nearly every waking hour of every day is affected by varied physical and emotional traumas. But as much as God cares about such traumas, that is not where he starts in offering comfort. He starts by comforting me/us in the face of the spiritual trauma of our sin. Notice his three comfort-promises in Isaiah 40:2.

1. Your warfare (primarily with and against God) is over. Our sins create conflict with, and warfare against God. But now he promises peace! This brings to mind Paul's words, "Therefore, since we have been justified by faith, we have peace with God through our Lord Jesus Christ" (Rom. 5:1).

2. Your sins (iniquities) are forgiven. Or again as Paul puts it, "In him we have redemption through his blood, the forgiveness of our trespasses, according to the riches of his grace" (Eph. 1:7). I am freely and fully forgiven; worthy of hell, but pardoned; sinful, but treated as sinless; truly guilty, but fully absolved; deserving of eternal chains forged by the wrath of God, but loosened and released into perfect freedom in the everlasting love of God. It's astonishing, and so very comforting!

3. Your debt has been paid. This is what "she has received from the Lord's hand double for all her sins" means. There had been a payment in full for the sins that they had committed.

Perfect and forever forgiveness, requires a perfect and forever sacrifice. The payment of the debt of our sins is what makes possible the forgiveness of our sins. God cannot merely wink at sin like an indulgent grandfather. He must punish it to make right what has been wrong.

But how is our debt paid? I don't think we can answer that unless we understand the forgiveness promise of Isaiah 40:2 in light of the atoning "offering-for-guilt" promise in Isaiah 53:4–12. That's where God promises the atoning sacrifice of Jesus, 700 years before Jesus was born.

> Surely he [Jesus, the Messiah] has borne our griefs and carried our sorrows . . . he was pierced for our transgressions; he was crushed for our iniquities; upon him was the chastisement that brought us peace, and with his wounds we are healed. All we like sheep have gone astray; we have turned—every one—to his own way; and the LORD has laid on him the iniquity of us all . . . although he had done no violence, and there was no deceit in his mouth. Yet it was the will of the LORD to crush him; he has put him to grief; when his soul makes an offering for guilt . . . by his knowledge shall the righteous one, my servant, make many to be accounted righteous, and he shall bear their iniquities. . . . he poured out his soul to death and . . . bore the sin of many, and makes intercession for the transgressors.

What awesome comfort! Jesus is the atoning offering for our sin. Jesus paid for all our sins by being pierced, crushed, chastised, put to grief, and poured out to death in our place. His punishment leads to our pardon.

And that's where the comfort of God begins; with God assuring us that he has paid our debt and forgiven everything. Whatever other sorrows we may face, none is greater than the guilt of our many, many sins. But this one thing we may know:

Jesus has borne them all away, which means there is a grace greater than all my sins.

Believe me, when you've had a brush with mortality such as I'm in the middle of right now, there is no comfort more comforting than this.

God Is on His Way

A voice cries:
"In the wilderness prepare the way of the LORD;
make straight in the desert a highway for our God."

Isaiah 40:3

God commanded long ago that a way *of* or *for* the Lord be prepared; and that a highway be straightened for him as our God. This is God's way of saying to his people, "Get ready! I'm coming to you and for you! I'm on the way!" Isn't that what ways and highways are for, to connect what is far apart?

When God inspired Isaiah's words about 2,700(+) years ago, he earnestly and tenderly comforted his people (Isa. 40:1–2) by predicting a "voice" crying in the wilderness that was going to prepare "the way of the LORD" and straighten a "highway for God."

This would have comforted Israel because they languished in Babylonian exile, feeling helplessly and hopelessly abandoned by God. But this verse is God's way of saying that he had not abandoned them, that he was going to return to them with his presence and power, and that they should get ready for it.

John the Baptist would turn out to be the primary fulfillment of this promised voice, crying in the wilderness. He was God's herald to get people ready for the first coming of Jesus (Matt. 3:1–3, 7–8; Mark 1:1–4; 11:7–10). With his voice he proclaimed the coming of the Messiah-Savior, Jesus Christ; announcing that God was and is on the move through the literal incarnation, perfect life, atoning death, bodily resurrection, glorious ascension, and ongoing triumphs of the Kingdom of God! Hallelujah!

In Day Four's meditation, I will note the imperative in our verse. But first, I find something comforting here; and I think it's the simple core comfort intended by God: God is coming for us! There is a "way of the LORD" and "highway for our God" that we are to prepare; presumably so that he can return and come to us on them. The coming King and Savior was (and is) on his way.

This says something about the character and heart of God: God is always on his way—taking the highway that connects where he is to where we are. Even in those moments when we feel like God is removed far from us, and is unapproachably distant from our personal spiritual exiles, he has a way and a highway that lead him to our side. He is coming to us and for us; which means that God is a God who comes; who arrives; who draws near; and who cries out to us, "Wait and watch for me, for I'm coming! I am on the way!"

This comfort in God's "coming" will be felt again when we

reflect on Isaiah 40:10–11: "Behold the Lord GOD *comes* [note that word!] with might . . . He will tend his flock like a shepherd; he will gather the lambs in his arms; he will carry them in his bosom, and gently lead those that are with young."

How wonderful! The Lord our God comes to us with a strong arm and in gentle care.

This is what I long to see now, with my own eyes in my own wilderness wanderings. So often it feels like God is on the other side of the cosmos; like he's abandoned me; like he's left me alone in my sorrows; like my diseases, losses, and multiplied sorrows are my own personal exile, with God being nowhere near.

But here he promises otherwise. There is "a way of the LORD . . . [and] in the desert, [there is] a highway for our God."

Of course, God is everywhere at the same time, and he is already right here as my "very present help in trouble" (Ps. 46:1). But he is also God-on-his-way, at all times. He is present and here in one sense, and he is soon-to-arrive in another. And at some point he will always come in such a way as to make that presence known and felt.

I can't speak for others, but in all that I am facing, I have no greater longing than to feel (yes, to feel, and not just to know) that he is coming and that he is near, here, and dear to my longing heart. Please Lord, you feel so far away. Please come to me and find me in my troubled place.

Leveling the Earth

"Every valley shall be lifted up,
    and every mountain and hill be made low;
the uneven ground shall become level,
    and the rough places a plain."

Isaiah 40:4

This is the time of the year when my friends post pictures of themselves hiking and climbing all over the globe. They seem determined to conquer whatever mountains and valleys they can.

One friend in particular fixates on rugged climbs and soaring heights. I've never forgotten how he planned such a Pennsylvania experience for a gathering of friends, including me; reassuring me that it was little more than a relaxed "walk in the woods." I had no idea that Kilimanjaro was in Pennsylvania. Who put that there?

I was done-in 10-15 minutes in, and found a nice cool place to rest until the others returned a couple hours later. And that was long before cancer and bone-disease. So no excuses. I've just always preferred walking on level ground. Ask me to reach a mountain peak, and I'll ask to be air-lifted.

I hope my mountain-climbing friends aren't saddened by today's text, and its prediction of a smooth and mountain-less world. You need not worry, it's not literal. Your mountains will remain intact forever. I'm sure that in the New Earth, there will be climbs and vistas to satisfy the most ardent mountaineer. Who knows, we might all become ardent mountaineers in heaven. I suspect we will!

But, I digress.

Our verse isn't about literal mountains. Rather, it's a symbolic expression of a spiritual imperative and promise. Spiritually speaking, the mountains *must* be leveled and the hills *will* be leveled.

Remember that verse 4 connects to verse 3, where we are told to prepare the way of the Lord and make straight his highway, so that he can come to us in power and grace. The way that we do that is by getting the mountains and valleys out of the way.

But what are the mountains and valleys? To understand, we'll need to think figuratively, by asking, "What are the dangerous mountains, dark valleys, rugged paths, perilous rocks, deadly cliffs, daunting heights, and crushing depths in our lives?

The answer is: our many sins.

God is calling us here to *repent* of the mountainous and cavernous sins that imperil our lives and get in the way of his coming favor. We are to raise dark sin-valleys and level high sin-mountains through the practice of repentance; lest sin hinder the coming blessing of God.

I say this because Mark says that John the Baptist was the voice in the wilderness that Isaiah predicted in Isaiah 40:3–4. John was the one who first prepared the way for the Lord's coming, and leveled the mountains and valleys so that the Messiah could come to bless. And he did this by "proclaiming a baptism of repentance for the forgiveness of sins" (see also Matt. 3:3, 8; Mark 1:2–5).

That's how John's father described John's ministry: "And you child, will be called the prophet of the Most High; for you will go before the Lord to prepare his ways, to give knowledge of salvation to his people in the forgiveness of their sins" (Luke 1:76–77).

John prepared his contemporaries for the Lord's coming favor by commanding (and practicing) repentance from sin so that they may be forgiven, and may experience the knowledge of salvation. And we prepare ourselves in the same way; by getting our sins out of the way.

We all have sin issues. Figuratively speaking, we've got sinful high mountains and deep valleys of which we need to repent if we want to be forgiven in order to receive God's fullest blessing. Repentance levels mountains of guilt, fills in valleys of shame, smooths over the rugged and rutted consequences of our sins, and opens the way for the salvation and blessing of God.

So where is the comfort in this? It is in the fact that God promises that "every mountain and valley (no matter how high or low) *shall*, in fact, be leveled." It shall be done. God will give us the gift of repentance and faith (as in 2 Tim. 2:24–25; Eph. 2:8–9) so that we may be fully forgiven and blessed by the coming Savior! We will be forgiven. We will be saved. We will be changed!

Be sure of it! God will get it done.

The Glory of the Lord

"And the glory of the LORD shall be revealed,
  and all flesh shall see it together,
  for the mouth of the LORD has spoken."

Isaiah 40:5

I could wish for the moment that I had James Earl Jones' boom-ing voice, and that—with a heart brimming with faith that God's words in Isaiah 40:5 are true (which faith I do have)—I could find a high mountain from which to herald forth this news. I want a voice to rattle the heavens and shake the very foundations of earth, space, and time—announcing the coming glory of God!

Repeat this verse ten times out loud and with faith and feel-ing. This is God's promise: that when Isaiah 40:3–4 happen, verse 5 will happen. When the sin-mountains and sin-valleys of our lives are leveled through repentance and God's forgiving grace, "Glory" will happen.

This leaves me with five questions.

1. What is glory? Glory is the shining or sounding forth of the inner worth, wonder, and weightiness of a being, object, or talent. The radiance of a noonday sun is its glory. The harmonies of transcendent singing voices are their glory. The thunderous roar of Niagara Falls is its glory. The vast, towering, and enduring strength of a Sequoia is its glory. Glory is that aspect of a sound or vision or character or skill that makes us say, "Wow" (or paradoxically, in reverent awe, say nothing at all).

2. What is the glory of the Lord? The "glory of the LORD" is the worth, wonder, and weightiness of his being on clear display; the shining forth of his majestic splendor, vast immensity, blazing beauty, infinite power, incomparable love, and undimmed holiness. It is the light, the sound, the splendor, and the majesty that Isaiah saw, heard, and felt in his famous vision of God in Isaiah 6:1–5. That's when the seraphim sang, "Holy, holy, holy is the LORD of hosts; the whole earth is full of his glory."

3. What is going to happen to that glory? "The glory of the LORD shall be revealed." Right now, though his glory can be seen in creation, in Christ, and even in our gradual transformation into his likeness (Ps. 19:1; Isa. 6:3; 2 Cor. 3:18; John 1:1, 14), it is veiled and mostly hidden from view. But in God's good time, as we repent to prepare a highway for our God and to level the sin-mountains and valleys of our hearts (see again Isa. 40:3–4), he is going to unveil his glory from one degree to another.

And at some point—and from then, right on through all eternity—we're all going to see Isaiah's vision on uninterrupted display forever and ever and ever!

4. Who will experience that glory? We are told that "All flesh shall see it (that glory) together." Similar to how every eye from horizon to horizon sees the lightening, even so, every eye in heaven above, on earth below, and in hell beneath, will behold the glory of God in Christ (Matt. 24:27, 30; Phil. 2:9–11; Rev. 1:5–8; 21:22–25); It will be a universal experience which for some will be utterly terrifying, and for others infinitely-satisfying.

In that moment, two things will vanish forever: both denial and doubt. Everyone will see the Glory, and no one will doubt again. For some that will mean eternal regret, and for others, everlasting joy.

5. How sure of this glory can we be? It is this sure: Isaiah says that "the mouth of the LORD has spoken," which is God's way to lock in as a sure thing what has been said. How can I be sure that God's glory will be revealed? I can be sure because God has spoken it with his own mouth, and whatever he says, he does.

So as sure as I am sitting here typing these words, the glory of God is going to be revealed with ever-increasing clarity and beauty, until the heavens open and we get lost in wonder, love, and praise.

Is there anything else for which to live? I do not think there is.

We Fading Flowers

A voice says, "Cry!"
  And I said, "What shall I cry?"
All flesh is grass,
  and all its beauty is like the flower of the field.

Isaiah 40:6

By all accounts, my hair has taken a recent definite turn toward the gray, and nothing but gray; a report confirmed by a look at last year's pictures and this year's mirror. Even worse, what is literally gray on my head is figuratively true everywhere else. My whole body is graying. Without a whisper of exaggeration, I've aged ten years in the past two. I am a fast-fading flower.

Consider Isaiah 40:6 which is part of a brief conversation between God and Isaiah, which I think may be paraphrased something like this:

GOD: "Isaiah, I want you to 'Cry' or 'Cry out' (for that is what I've called you to do)!"

ISAIAH: "But LORD, what shall I cry out?"

(??): "All flesh is grass, and all its beauty is like the flower of the field."

Since there are no punctuation marks in the ancient Hebrew text, it's hard to tell if the statement after Isaiah's "What shall I cry out?" is God's or the prophet's. If it's God's, God is telling Isaiah what to say (i.e., to tell people that, in effect they are nothing but sun-withered grass and sun-wilted flowers at high noon in a wilderness during a heat spell).

But if it's Isaiah's statement, he's telling God that there hardly seems any point to crying out to tell the people anything. After all, his hearers were little more than sun-withered human grass and sun-wilted flowers who seemed hardly worth the effort.

Whatever the case, what we have here is an accurate description of our human condition: We are sun-withered grass and fading flowers.

There's more to this in Isaiah 40:7–8. But for now, I am struck by this simple statement: "*All* flesh (i.e., every single human being) is grass, and *all its beauty* (i.e., all human existence, looks, vigor and vitality, power, accomplishment, greatness, and alleged beauty) is a fast-fading flower.

This brings to mind a series of similar texts that warn of the fleeting existence of man:

- "Man is like a breath; his days are like a fleeting shadow" (Ps. 144:4)
- Man's life can be measured with a twelve-inch ruler (two hand-breadths) (Ps. 39:4–6)

- "All [man's] days pass away ... they are soon gone, and we fly away" (Ps. 90:9–10)
- [On a balance scale] man's side "goes up" while the empty side goes down (Ps. 62:9)
- "[Man's life is] but a mist that appears for a little time and then vanishes" (James 4:14b)

So, I am but a fading flower, a fleeting shadow, a morning mist, a weightless lighter-than-air wisp, and a mere breath.

There will be more of this in upcoming reflections, but I need to pause to ask, "How is this comforting? Isn't Isaiah 40 supposed to be about God comforting us as his people?"

Yes, it is.

And this *is* comforting if we remember who Israel was up against. They were facing angry godless hordes of Babylonians with seemingly boundless power and absolute control. The Babylonians boasted of their beauty and flaunted their power (much like tyrants, politicians, power-brokers and modern villains do today). But in truth they—back then and now—are mere passing mortals whom we need not fear. They are no more than withering weeds and wilting flowers.

This is also comforting because it puts me and my doubly-diseased life into perspective. It reminds me that we are all fading flowers; that in the end we're all mortal; and that my illnesses and prognoses do not make me different from, or worse off, than anyone else. They simply prove that in myself, I am little more than passing tumbleweed.

It is good for me to remember my mortality, number my days, visit funeral homes (Eccel. 7:2–4), learn wisdom (Ps.

90:12), and, in the words of one man, "live on the edge of eternity, being packed up and ready to go." I don't know who first said it, but I'll echo it here and now: No man is rightly prepared to live who is not first, prepared to die.

Isaiah 40:6 and my cancer remind me that my flower is fading fast; and I am the better off for knowing that it is so.

The Hot Breath of God

The grass withers, the flower fades
when the breath of the LORD blows on it;
surely the people are grass.

Isaiah 40:7

Two days ago (July 13, 2024), we witnessed a man's brush with death. A former President's ear was bloodied by a sniper's passing bullet. Yet, amazingly, he survived. An inch more to the left and the man would have died. Mortality knocked on the door, and then in a split second passed him by.

Frankly speaking, mortality knocks on every door, every day. The repeated couplet in today's Isaiah 40 text (and many other texts) says that it is so:

- "All flesh is grass ... The grass withers, the flower fades" (Isa. 40:6–7a)
- "The people are grass ... The grass withers, the flower fades (Isa. 40:7–8)

Everyone is as grass. And the grass withers and the flower

fades. This teaches me four truths about my mortality:

1. Mortality is universal. *All flesh* is as withered grass and a fading flower. No exceptions.

2. Mortality is humbling. Just like flowers are the glory and beauty of the grass of the field, and yet they perish in a day, even so death is the fading and withering of the human flower (Isa. 28:3–4). Our mortality is the fading of the beauty and glory of man; the humbling of our vaunted knowledge and power.

As James puts it so clearly, "[The rich should be happy when he is humbled] because like a flower of the grass he will pass away. For the sun rises with its scorching heat and withers the grass; its flower falls, and its beauty perishes. So, also will the rich man fade away in the midst of his pursuits" (James 1:10–11).

Whatever we think of our former President, we should be grateful that he survived and then pray that he will be humbled by it all. Indeed, one hopes that we all will be humbled by it all. For if we are not humbled to acknowledge our utter dependence upon God in this life, we will be humbled in the life to come. It's all so sobering.

3. Mortality is imposed by God. When the hot "breath of the Lord" blows on us we fade and wither. God decides our time. And as for me, God will decide *my* time. Not a cancer. Not a heart attack. Not a car accident. Not a sniper or drive-by shooter. Not an overdose. I will die when the hot breath of God breathes upon the mortal flesh that is my body. Precisely then it will be over. Not a moment sooner or a second later.

The mystery of mortality is that while this week's sniper missed his mark by an inch, countless bullets, diseases, and deadly accidents have not. I recall that, world-wide, 150,000 people die every day. That's 104 people every minute (the time it took me to type the last two paragraphs). One man lives, 150,000 die. A sovereign Creator-God's all-wise plan decides.

4. Mortality is near. Isaiah says that the flower fades in a hurry. And he is not alone in saying this:

- "Man who is born of a woman is few in days and full of trouble. He comes out like a flower and withers; he flees like a shadow and continues not" (Job 14:1–2)
- "As for man, his days are like grass; he flourishes like a flower of the field; for the wind passes over it, and it is gone, and its place knows it no more" (Ps. 103:15–16)

I put it like this:

The truth is this, we're fading fast;

Scorched by God-Almighty's blast.

Such fearful language about God (and our mortality) is meant to humble us, and lead us to repentance and salvation in Christ; the one in whom we may have eternal life. God's warnings are mercies, to call us to repent and believe. For in Christ we are immortal, and the flaming breath of God will never consume us.

In our Lord's own words, "I am the resurrection and the life. Whoever believes in me, though he die, yet shall he live; and everyone who lives and believes in me shall never die. Do you believe this" (John 11:25–26)?

Christ reverses death. Do you believe? Do I? Today's text and this week's events should make us all stop to consider our mortality and eternity before the clock strikes midnight.

The Abiding Word

The grass withers, the flower fades,
   but the word of our God will stand forever.

Isaiah 40:8

The verse that I just typed—and each word within that verse—
is the word of God. Likewise, the whole Bible from which I took
that verse, is also the word of God.

The *word of God* can be either a single word spoken by God,
or it can be the singular unified whole of God's Word. We might
call this "God's Three-Volume Word: Nature, Scripture, and
Manger" (i.e., the incarnation of the Son of God, who was and
is God's final Word (Ps. 19:1; John 1:1, 14; 2 Tim. 3:16–17; Heb.
1:1–2). God's word is the all-sufficient and infallible record of
every needed thing that God has ever said to us; which is most
perfectly summarized and preserved in the Bible.

There are two great realities in Isaiah 40:8 that need to
shape my life:

1. Humans are like grass, and all our glory, beauty,
   vaunted opinions, and many words are but flowers

that fade under the scorching sun.

2.   God's word stands forever, as the very opposite of fast-fading human words or worth. So there's every reason to love and trust it without doubt or debate. Everything that man says, is, and does, withers in a moment. Everything that God says, is, and does, stands forever.

God's "word" means that God **speaks**.

That God has a "word" means that God has *spoken* (Isa. 40:5). That helps those of us who've wondered why God doesn't open his mouth and say something. He seems so distant and silent. But he is neither. God has spoken and revealed himself to us in Nature, Scripture, and Manger. Which means, when I think about it, that not only does God speak; he never stops talking!

God's word is the word of **our** God.

The God who speaks is *our* God who invites us to hear his voice as the voice of him who has made us his own, and has allowed us to claim him as our own. That the word of God is the word of OUR God means that his word is personal, relational, and full of love. It means that when I ponder his word, God is speaking to me; and yes, to you as well. It means that we are hearing what is on his mind and in his heart, in our behalf and for our joy.

God's word will **stand**.

God's word is established. It is firm, fixed, and final. It doesn't wobble, teeter, stumble, or fall. It is always on its feet. What a contrast to me! My overweight and doubly-diseased body is wobbly and unsteady. When I try to get on my feet, it's just not fair to them! They hardly have a chance. So I've got to plant my feet securely in place, so they can hold me up under the stress of it all. Still, I wobble and teeter. But God's word stands.

God's word will stand **forever.**

God's word will never wobble, teeter, or fall, but will stand tall right on into and throughout eternity. As the psalmist says, "Forever O LORD, your word is firmly fixed in the heavens" (Ps. 119:89)!

God's word is not like the words, thoughts, and opinions of frail human flowers. Rather, like a giant Sequoia or mighty redwood, it stands firm and is forever fixed, towering into the heavens. There—where no human power or vain boast or empty words can rival it—it will stand forever, without failing or falling.

Peter celebrates these same truths by citing our Isaiah 40 text: "[Y]ou have been born again, not of perishable seed but of imperishable, through the living and abiding word of God, for 'all flesh is like grass and all its glory like the flower of grass. The grass withers and the flower falls, but the word of the Lord remains forever'" (1 Peter 1:23–25).

Yes, it does.

I find this so comforting in this age of fake news and deliberate misinformation and disinformation. We just don't know whom we can trust. But we have a sure word of truth. To the everlasting praise of God, we know that he has spoken, and that the Bible is the one Book that endures, the one source of information that is dependable, and the one word of truth that can be trusted.

It never fails.

Behold Your God

Go on up to a high mountain,
  O Zion, herald of good news
lift up your voice with strength,
  O Jerusalem, herald of good news;
  lift it up, fear not;
say to the cities of Judah,
  "Behold your God!"

Isaiah 40:9

These are pretty exhilarating words, given the somewhat somber reputation of Old Testament prophets. Wouldn't you agree? But the truth is, that the prophet had something exhilaratingly awesome to herald to his generation. God's people who had suffered so much, were now being invited into the greatest comfort there is.

We must keep in mind that comfort is the whole point of Isaiah 40. God wants to console his people (Isa. 40:1–2). And in arriving at Isaiah 40:9 it's time for the primary focus of that comfort to be revealed. So God gives Isaiah some specific directions for delivering it.

1. God identifies Isaiah. Twice he calls the prophet, who is a voice for Zion and Jerusalem, a "herald of good news," the one with the privilege of standing up before others and ringing forth just about the best good news that's ever been proclaimed.

2. God tells Isaiah where to stand. "Isaiah: Go up on a high mountain where your voice can boom for all to hear. What I want you to herald is too good to whisper in secret with a covered mouth."

3. God tells Isaiah whom to address. "Isaiah: Speak to the cities of Judah who have seen so much sorrow and are surrounded by enemies, to remind them of my comfort."

4. God tells Isaiah how to speak. "Isaiah: Herald the good news 'with strength and without fear.' Be so invigorated by this good news, that you'll be strong and fearless to tell everyone."

5. God tells Isaiah what to say. "Isaiah: Tell the people the good news that they can—and need to—behold their God, whom I am about to reveal in all the verses that follow. In other words, tell them that I am the good news!"

To comfort his people, God tells Isaiah to tell the people to behold him.

This one charge—"Behold your God"—which is gloriously expanded in the vision that follows, has been heaven's comforting lifeline for my soul hundreds of times. In part this has been through *hearing* his words and *receiving* his promised blessings. But mostly, it's been through *seeing* who he is. The grandeur of God in Isaiah 40:9–31 is meant to comfort God's people.

With some indebtedness to Charles Spurgeon's style (and a little bit to his content), I wrote the following many years ago.

Nothing so restores the ruined, so strengthens the weak, so comforts the sorrowful, so lifts the fallen, so sustains the infirmed, so raises the downcast, so binds up the broken, so heals the wounded, so satisfies the hungry, so dignifies the downtrodden, so sanctifies the wayward, so comforts the headache, and, yes, so quells the cancer-induced fear. as does a frequent, persistent, life-long gaze of the soul upon the being and beauty of God. If you want grace for all of life, make an adoring vision of God the daily impassioned pursuit of your life (for Mr. Spurgeon's version see J.I. Packer, *Knowing God*, Chapter One).

If I believed this years ago when my sorrows were fewer and lighter, I must, and I still do believe it, today. I must, for all other comforts are in vain.

Put simply: to behold God is to know that we are beheld by him. To see God is to know that he sees us. To gaze upon the beauty of God is to be made beautiful in his likeness. To worship the glory of God is to be made glorious. To encounter the holiness of God is to be made more holy. To feel the love of God is to be filled with that love.

Later on in Isaiah, God says, "How beautiful upon the mountains are the feet of him who brings good news, who publishes peace, who brings good news of happiness, who publishes salvation, who says to Zion, 'Your God reigns'" (Isa. 52:7).

"Behold your God" and "Your God reigns." That's some of

the best news ever. To be comforted we are invited to behold the God who reigns over all that is—including our laments and losses—for our gladness and his glory, forever.

So may whoever needs to be comforted "Behold their God"—and be comforted today. And then, may they get up and go, to tell it on a high mountain!

He Comes with Might

Behold, the Lord GOD comes with might,
and his arm rules for him;
behold, his reward is with him,
and his recompense before him.

Isaiah 40:10

When we, like Israel of old, face fierce enemies, gross injustices, immense wrongs, and profound loss, we need to view God with telescopic vision to see his expanding glory.

"Behold."

"Behold the Lord GOD."

"Behold the Lord GOD [who] comes."

"Behold the Lord GOD [who] comes with might."

"Behold the Lord GOD [who] comes with might and his arm rules for him."

"Behold the Lord GOD [whose] reward is with him, and his recompense before him."

Three Great Comforts

There are three great comforts in beholding God as he is in Isaiah 40:10.

1. The first comfort is that God will make all things right. Here is comfort for the downtrodden, abused, betrayed, unjustly accused, abandoned, and innocently afflicted. God will give those who have sinned against us their due, and will even the score.

This doesn't allow us to wish vindictively for others to be punished (for Jesus teaches us to pray for and do good to our enemies (Matt. 5:44–48; Luke 6:35). But it is to say that if we have prayed that our enemies would be saved and blessed, but they refuse to repent, apologize, or make things right, we need not grow bitter or angry. Instead we may know that they won't get away with it, because God will take care of it.

2. The second comfort is that we don't have to make all things right. We can let God do that. As Paul writes: "Beloved, never avenge yourselves, but leave it to the wrath of God, for it is written, 'Vengeance is mine, I will repay, says the Lord'" (Rom. 12:19).

We need to believe that God's justice, however long delayed, is on the way. And even though justice-closure seldom happens in this life, we must not be embittered, and we must be willing to wait. The Final Day will bring all things to light.

Nothing else comforts me or gives me hope in the face of global bullies, political abuses of power, rampant injustice, violent evil-doers, and Satan's fierce attacks against my health and happiness. If a real wrong is done, God has written it down, and he will make it right. Only usually, not right now. For reasons which God alone knows, justice may have to wait. But God will make it right, and we can leave it there.

3. The third comfort is that God will reward all those who have done well. Isaiah 40:10 is not just about the punishment of wrongdoers. It is also about the reward of those who do right. The Mighty Judge is also a Merciful Judge who will reward our faithfulness and obedience in the face of injustice, suffering, sickness, and hardship.

I was lying in bed last night, feeling unfairly treated. Healing for my jaw disease is still far off (and I wonder what I did to deserve this). My doctor told me yesterday that I'll have to carry my ball-and-chain intravenous pump and medical fanny pack around for a minimum of six more weeks, and quite possibly more. Do you know that by the time this jaw disease is fully cured (if that even happens) it will have consumed a full year and a half of my life; one of the few years that I have left, if cancer does its normal usual worst?

It seems unfair.

Plus, while my cancer seems on hold, and doctors are saying that I could live a while longer, that "living" includes treatment-caused relentless pain, weakness, disability, and sorrow. So if treatments give me a few extra years of life, what are they giving me, except a few more years of painful exhausting trouble?

That's my grief talking there. I know. But I do wonder why God allows it all. It just doesn't seem fair that I am facing so much. It's enough to make me cry, and it often has.

But if I believe that God is permitting these trials for his all-wise reasons, I can choose to submit willingly to them for Jesus's sake, that I might suffer well for his glory and be able to comfort others through my afflictions. And if I do not accuse God of wrong-doing and injustice, but humbly resign myself to his will in faith and in hope, then I will receive my reward.

Alright then, my Lord. I surrender.

But only because I believe that the reward promised in Isaiah 40:10 is real.

Otherwise I'd be sad and mad like nobody's business.

But, I do surrender, because you have promised and cannot lie.

He Will Tend His Flock

He will tend his flock like a shepherd;
  he will gather the lambs in his arms;
he will carry them in his bosom,
  and gently lead those that are with young.

Isaiah 40:11

Of all the comforting texts of Scripture, this may be the most tenderly affecting there is. Oh that we all might feel it deeply! But for that to happen we need to see ourselves as "harassed and helpless" sheep; vulnerable scattered lambs just like the exiled ancient people of God were (Isa. 39:5–7; Matt. 9:36).

We cannot think of ourselves as strong or self-sufficient. We are not charging bulls or roaring lions or stampeding horses. We are broken and bloodied lambs, limping on fractured legs, with tangled and matted wool, thorn-shredded sides, and mud-caked bodies from head to hoof. And that sound of bleating cries for help? That's us, when far from the Shepherd's fold.

That is really how I see myself these days. Emotionally and

physically, I'm a broken, bloodied, and bleating lamb. And spiritually, I'm a mud-caked sinner who sometimes feels so far from Home that I wonder if I'll ever make the return trip. Oh how I need the gentle, good, and great Shepherd of the sheep (Ps. 23; John 10:1–16; Heb. 13:20). And how I would weep with joy to see my Shepherd now; just as he is!

But in the meantime, we all must find comfort in these four promises:

1. The Shepherd will attentively provide for us. That's what it means to "tend." Jesus feeds, cares for, protects and provides—so that we can sing with David, "The LORD is my Shepherd, I shall not want" (Ps. 23:1). Indeed, no good thing will our Shepherd withhold from us (Ps. 84:11).

2. The Shepherd will patiently gather us. To make sure that there won't be any stragglers, wanderers, or lambs left behind, Jesus will find each of us in our lost and lonely places, and gather each of us up into his strong arms.

3. The Shepherd will tenderly carry us. He will carry us in his bosom. This is language of affection and tender love. When tired and broken sheep like us are so wearied as to hardly walk, he will lift us and hold us close. I especially love how our God says he will gently carry "the lambs" and "those with young" (i.e., little ones and nursing moms). What care he has for the dearest and most vulnerable among us!

4. The Shepherd will gently lead us. Unlike tyrants like Babylon's Nebuchadnezzar who *drove* the Israelites from their home, Jesus our Shepherd promises to lead us gently, and to pick us up to *carry* us home. Because ancient Israel was exiled to Babylon they needed to know that God was there, too. He was there as their Shepherd, and so his tending, gathering, hugging and leading grace was always there, too.

Desert exile did not imply a deserting God. God was close though he seemed far. And he urged the prophet to comfort his people with the promise that he would be right there with them—leading and carrying them all the way back to his fold again.

We've all experienced the chasm between what is promised and what we feel. I cannot pretend otherwise. I long to feel the gentle care that Isaiah 40:11 promises, but in this recent season not much of what I've experienced has felt very gentle or tender. I've had debilitating cancer treatments, a screaming case of poison ivy, and a prolonged agonizing jawbone disease with pain sometimes equal to a couple cavities and root canals (not to mention many other losses and crosses). If this is how gentle and tender feel, I'd hate to feel harsh and hard.

But such are times when I need to believe what I cannot see. I need to pray for what my own weary and beleaguered heart cannot feel:

Dear Shepherd, just as you have promised, please provide for me attentively, gather me up patiently, carry me close tenderly, and lead me on gently. I know that I am safe in your arms Gentle Jesus, for you have assured me of your tender care, and I know you cannot lie. I know, too, that one day I will look back and see how you were right there with me every step of the journey Home. But please Lord Jesus, help me to feel more of that right now. Amen.

The Scales of God

Who has measured the waters in the hollow of his hand
  and marked off the heavens with a span,
enclosed the dust of the earth in a measure
  and weighed the mountains in scales
  and the hills in a balance?

Isaiah 40:12

Isaiah 40 is all about the *attributes of God*; which is a term/phrase that is too seldom heard nowadays. An attribute of God is more than a characteristic of God. It is an *essential* part or necessary perfection of his being; a quality without which he would not be the true and living God that he is.

I see three attributes of God in this one verse:

1. His vast immensity. God cups his hands and scoops up all the water on earth. He is so immense that one span of his hand—the distance from the tip of his thumb to the tip of his pinky—can measure all the heavens. God can number all the specks of dust and grains of sand, as if holding them in a measuring cup. And he can lift the mountains and weigh them on his scales.

All this figurative language clearly speaks of the vast immensity of God. He is the one who "is high and lifted up, who inhabits eternity" (Isa. 57:15), who asks with all self-assurance, "Do I not fill heaven and earth," and who declares heaven to be his throne, and the earth his footstool (Isa. 66:1; Jer. 23:24). As one has put it, "The world dwarfs us all, but God dwarfs the world" (J.I. Packer, *Knowing God*).

2. His all-encompassing knowledge. Our text is not just about the vast immensity of God, it is also about his all-encompassing knowledge. Our verse sounds like God is taking inventory of everything in the cosmos, and getting every spreadsheet right.The point is that he actually knows how many pounds the mountains weigh, how many grains of sand and specks of dust are on the earth, how many inches, feet, miles, and light-years span the galaxies, how many gallons or cups or spoonfuls of water are in the ocean, how many stars are in the cosmos, and, for that matter, how many hairs are on each and every one of our heads (Isa. 40:12, 26; Matt. 10:30).

I like how the New Living Translation puts it:

> Who else has held the oceans in his hand?
>> Who else has measured off the heavens with his fingers?
> Who else knows the weight of the earth
>> Or has weighed the mountains and hills on a scale?

The flurry of rhetorical questions assumes that God has done all these things, and that no one else ever has, or ever could.

3. His providential care. That God has actually taken inventory of all that is in his cosmos indicates that it all matters to him, and falls under the oversight of his providential care. That he has "bothered to count" the grains of sand and weigh the mountains shows that this is his world after all, and that everything in it belongs to him (Ps. 24:1–2). He's keeping watchful care over all his creatures to provide every need they have. Oh how good this is to know (Ps. 104:1–35 celebrates this providential care beautifully)!

Is My God Too Small?

Isaiah 40:12 addresses my biggest faith problem. It reminds me that often my thoughts of God are too small. It reminds me of why I doubt and fear so much; why I sometimes feel isolated from God's care; and why I ever have even a hint of worry about tomorrow. It's because I've have lost sight of the vastness and nearness of God.

In truth, I'm not the only one with a faith problem. If people are doubting God, or are mad at God, or are indifferent toward God, or are feeling like God is distant and disinterested while they're afflicted with many and varied sorrows, it is because their God is too small. They haven't seen his immensity yet, or plumbed the depths of his unfathomable knowledge yet, or remembered yet that he numbers and cares for their every need.

I need to recall this when all goes wrong in my minuscule corner of the universe. I need to remember with hope—and I will—that God occupies both my little space and all of outer space, and that he is vast in his immensity, all-encompassing in his knowledge, and ever-faithful and unfailing in his providential care.

Amen.

The Sovereign Spirit

Who has measured the Spirit of the LORD,
or what man shows him his counsel?

Isaiah 40:13

Each of these rhetorical questions has an assumed answer of "no one" and "no man," and both of them are meant to comfort us in our troubles (Isa. 40:1–2). And I need that comfort badly.

Yesterday I felt like I was gut-punched; as if, out of nowhere my body got pummeled and left for dead. I don't know if it was a several-hour wave of treatment side-effects, or a medication reaction, or a sudden cancer punch, or simply the intense cumulative effect on my headache that my hundred stresses a day tend to have. All I know is that it cast a sudden devastating pall over everything.

But this morning, Isaiah 40:13 is helping me rise to my feet—even if a bit battered and bloodied. Here's what I'm seeing.

1. The Spirit of the Lord cannot be measured. To be measured implies limitations of time, space, size, power, love, or wisdom. If you've measured Tim Shorey, it means that you've reached the end of him. You have found that he is six-feet-four-inches tall and 250++ pounds wide. Measure Tim's energy supply, and you'll find me limited even when full, and nearly empty all the time. To be measured is to be finite and limited.

In contrast to all of us, the Spirit of the Lord is infinite. He is a boundless, limitless, endless, and measureless Spirit-Person who cannot be calculated by human metrics, weights, or scales; but rather occupies infinity in every sense of the word.

2. The Spirit of the Lord submits to no one. Part of the meaning of the Hebrew word translated measured is the idea of being "measured out" or meted out and apportioned. In other words, Isaiah asks: "Who has divided up and meted out the Spirit as if he were ours to direct, distribute, or tell where to go or what to do?" No one.

The Spirit of the Lord is a sovereign Spirit who goes wherever he wishes, and blows the wind of his powerful grace as he sees fit. He cannot be weighed, measured, apportioned, or distributed by anyone.

Jesus affirms this when he said, "The wind blows where it wishes, and you hear its sound, but you do no know where it comes from or where it goes. So it is with everyone who is born of the Spirit" (John 3:8).

The Spirit who creates, regenerates, heals, gifts, fills, and empowers, submits to no one. He has his own mind and charts his own course (Gen. 1:1–2; 1 Cor. 12:4–11).

3. The Spirit of the Lord doesn't need my advice. Likewise, the Spirit of the Lord does not need my advice. Isaiah 40:13

asks, "What man shows him his counsel?" In other words: Who can give advice to God, the Holy Spirit? No one. He knows everything and he knows best. So what does he need my two cents for? Absolutely nothing at all.

Somehow it's comforting to know that God the Holy Spirit functions at an infinitely higher level than me, and does not need my input. As God will say later, "My thoughts are not your thoughts, neither are your ways my ways, declares the LORD. For as the heavens are higher than the earth, so are my ways higher than your ways and my thoughts than your thoughts" (Isa. 55:8–9). That's all I need to know.

And so the Spirit of the Lord cannot be measured, submits to no one, and does not need my advice, which means that he is infinite in his Person, sovereign in his purposes, and all-wise in his plans. If I want comfort in my troubles, I simply must believe that it is so.

Time is teaching me that while lament is valid and essential, I have to choose my way out of it. I cannot let grief master me. I have to choose every day (1) to trust in the immeasurable sovereign Spirit, who is free to come and go as he pleases; (2) to cover my mouth when I think my ideas are better than his; and (3) to rest securely in his all-knowing reasons.

John Piper is wise in writing, "Occasionally weep deeply over the life you hoped would be. Grieve the losses. Then wash your face. Trust God. And embrace the life you have" (John Piper, "Embrace the Life God Has Given You," video).

Holy Spirit of God, please help me do that today.

The God with Nothing to Learn

Whom did he consult,
  and who made him understand?
Who taught him the path of justice,
  and taught him knowledge,
  and showed him the way of understanding?

Isaiah 40:14

I have another new doctor's appointment next week. This time it's a gastroenterologist who is going to thread a tube-light down my throat to look around for whatever's causing the cough that has been hounding me for the past year.

Funny thing about all my doctors. They never know anything without some kind of process to figure out what it is. I've never had a doctor just look at me and say, "Tim, you have cancer" or "You have a jaw-bone disease," or "You have New Daily Persistent Headache (yes, that is a thing)," or "You have three herniated discs," or "You have _____ which is causing your every day year-long cough."

I do have all these, but not one doctor knew I had them

without help. Doctors guess, rely on tests, and in many cases, consult with specialists. And even then they often get it wrong. Think about it: where would medical care be without blood tests, X-rays, MRIs, bone scans, biopsies, endoscopies, (and even pregnancy tests)?

The truth is that we all are information-dependent. We rely completely on outside sources to know anything at all. I've never known anything by pure intuition. Nobody knows anything without being taught it, or having a test done to discover it, or completing the due process that proves it, or attending life's "school of hard knocks" to experience it.

Meanwhile, God just knows.

Apart from multiple outside sources, I know nothing. Yet, without any outside sources, God knows everything.

Today's Isaiah text combines five rapid-fire rhetorical questions to celebrate God's perfect unlearned knowledge of all things—his infallible omniscience, wisdom, and justice—all to comfort our woefully ignorant hearts:

1. Who has been God's consultant-advisor? (No one)
2. Who has helped God to understand something better? (No one)
3. Who has schooled God in the path of justice? (No one)
4. Who has taught God anything that he didn't already know? (Not one person), and
5. Who has shown God the way of wise understanding? (Not a single solitary soul)

God is utterly independent and self-sufficient in his knowledge. Nobody has ever given God advice. No one has ever deepened his understanding. Nobody has ever sharpened his intellect. Nobody has ever taught God justice or disproven him in a court of law. Nobody has ever filled in any gaps in God's knowledge. Nobody has ever pulled him aside to remind him of things he's ignored or forgotten. Nobody has ever improved upon his wisdom. And nobody has ever corrected him correctly.

He is the God who has never, ever, ever had anything to learn.

This is what we mean by God's omniscience. His knowledge is unlimited. Past events, present circumstances, future certainties and possibilities, and every single need and sorrow of his people in between: God knows them all. You cannot teach God anything, because he already knows everything. *"His understanding is unsearchable"* (Isa. 40:28). This means that we simply cannot fathom the depths of what God knows. Incomprehensible as it is to us, nothing is incomprehensible to God (Job 21:22; Isa. 40:13–14; Rom. 11:33–34).

When I question God or doubt that he sees or cares, I am doubting the omniscience of God. When I wonder if my way is "hidden from the LORD" and my rights are being disregarded by him, I am suggesting that it is possible for something to happen behind God's back in God's universe without God knowing (Isa. 40:27–28). But that cannot be. Not one of our world's crises, or our own personal needs, or desperate wants or blazing hurts, or perceived injustices has escaped the notice of God's all seeing and knowing eye. He is surprised by nothing because he sees everything, every moment, everywhere—even before it happens (Isa. 44:6–8).

How I thank God once again for his attributes! For when we know that God knows everything without ever being taught anything—and that he is infallibly wise and just in that knowledge—we can know that everything is going to be okay. It means that whenever we go to God with any concern, he is already "on it," since he knew about it without having to be told (Matt. 6:7–8).

How great is this God who is watching out for us!

The Nations Matter Nothing to God's Existence

Behold, the nations are like a drop from a bucket,
and are accounted as the dust on the scales;
behold, he takes up the coastlands like fine dust.

Isaiah 40:15

The next few Isaiah 40 verse-by-verse reflections are about how God views all the nations on earth.

This could hardly be more timely, since we're in the middle of an abominable election cycle during which godless people on all sides are pursuing national power while showing no sign of genuinely pursuing God, or bowing before his throne.

To accent all the nations' proud obsession with national achievement, power, and dominance, we're also in mid-Olympics season; an every-four-year moment when all the nations of earth throw an aren't-we-wonderful pride parade, and are almost completely godless in the process.

Don't get me wrong. I enjoy seeing human achievement expressed in beauty, skill, sport, art, and culture. Being made in the image of God, we are capable of many wonderful achievements that are worth enjoying. But God intends that every human capacity and activity, right down to mere eating and drinking, be done to the glory of God alone (1 Cor. 10:31). Maybe I missed it, but I'm not sensing much glory-of-God motivation behind our politics or the Olympics. Did I miss an opening ceremony prayer offered to the true and living God, giving him glory for all things? I don't think so.

The nations of this world (which include various ethnicities, cultures, colors, tribes, and other political-cultural entities) do all they do for the glory of self. And then they flaunt their power, go to war, oppress the poor, boast in their sins, and, as happened with Babylon's attack on ancient Israel, turn their hatred upon God's people; defying the Lord of the nations as if he doesn't exist.

This makes God's comfort to Israel relevant for us. Here are his four reminders:

- The Nations Matter Nothing to God's Existence (Isa. 40:15)
- The Nations Contribute Nothing to God's Existence (Isa. 40:16)
- The Nations Are Less Than Nothing When Compared to God's Existence (Isa. 40:17)
- The Nations Can Do Nothing without God's Existence (Isa. 40:23–24)

I wonder how often I've spilled a drop of water. Of course, there is no way to know unless I have cared enough to stop, notice, and count. And that's not happening. And why not? Because a spilled drop of water matters nothing.

If you're wondering how inconsequential the nations are to God, consider this: "Behold, the nations are like a drop from a bucket" (Isa. 40:15). That's either a drop from a bucket or a drop in a bucket. Either way works. When a drop falls into or out of a bucket, it is utterly inconsequential. It doesn't matter one single bit.

And that is how God views the nations. They matter nothing to his existence. Which means that the nation, culture, ethnicity, and national power and prowess of which we are so very proud, are but a drop. And all those many nations, political parties and global entities of which are so afraid? They, too, are drops of insignificance to God.

God comforts ancient Israel in her political trauma and global upheaval by reminding her that all the nations are but a drop from a bucket. They are like a fistful of dust that he casts to the wind (Isa. 40:15).

To say that the nations do not matter to God's *existence* doesn't mean that that they don't matter to his *heart.* God cares deeply about the nations; so much so that one day he will redeem sinners from every nation on earth (Isa. 2:2–4; 19:19–25; 49:6; 52:10; 60:1–3; 66:18–23; Rev. 5:9–10). Indeed, they matter much to his heart.

But still: they matter nothing to his existence. He is utterly independent of them.

And that means that the nations mean nothing without his giving them a meaningful reason to exist. Babylon, Democrat-led America, Republican-led America, China, Egypt, Iran, North Korea, Al Qaeda, White Nationalist terrorists, or Antifa extremists are all insignificant national, ethnic, tribal driblets that will evaporate before they hit the ground—as soon as God's purposes for them are complete.

It all begs the question: If this is so when it comes to the nations, why are we so proud of ours and afraid of theirs?

More to come.

The Nations Contribute Nothing to God's Existence

Lebanon would not suffice for fuel,
nor are its beasts enough for a burnt offering.

Isaiah 40:16

The prophet is comforting God's people, as commanded in Isaiah 40:1. As it turns out, that comfort includes some unflattering reflections on the nations of this world (Isa. 40:15–17, 23–24). This seems like counter intuitive comfort to me, since normally, we citizens derive comfort by taking refuge in a strong national defense, a strong economy, a strong set of allies.

But in Isaiah 40 God exposes the nations for the imposters that they are. In God's view, nations are part of the problem, not the solution. Nations come and go. Only God endures forever. In truth, nations are too weak to be trusted, too wicked to be admired, and too inconsequential to be feared.

In Isaiah 40:15–24, God taunts the nations in order to comfort us. When the nation of Babylon invaded and left Israel's nation in ruins (Isa. 39:5–7), it felt like the whole world was crumbling around them. So God reminds Israel (and us) that he is Lord over the nations, and that they are nothing.

That's why God reminded them that "Lebanon would not suffice for fuel, nor ... its beasts ... for a burnt offering" (Isa. 40:16).

Lebanon was a thickly forested nation abounding in the fuel needed for burnt offerings presented to God. But even its vast supply of trees wasn't enough. The same was true for Lebanon's beasts. There simply weren't enough of them to offer adequate sacrifices to God.

This means that Lebanon's boasted best was worthless to God. What Lebanon thought it could offer to God, contributed nothing to him at all. And how could it, since the cedars and beasts of Lebanon were already God's to begin with?

That's how God argues elsewhere—"I will not accept a bull from your house or goats from your folds. For every beast of the forest is mine, the cattle on a thousand hills. I know all the birds of the hills, and all that moves in the field is mine. If I were hungry, I would not tell you, for the world and its fullness are mine" (Ps. 50:9–13). Left to themselves, humans have nothing to offer to God, nothing of any real value to contribute.

And nations don't either. God doesn't create nations because he needs them. Their resources—whether trees and technology, or beasts and bombs, or armies and strategies—cannot help God's cause in any way. God may choose to use a nation for a temporary purpose but he absolutely never will need one.

We need God. He doesn't need us. Dependence is a one way

street from earth to heaven. As Paul declares, "The God who made the world and everything in it, being Lord of heaven and earth, does not live in temples made by man, nor is he served by human hands, as though he needed anything, since he himself gives to all mankind life and breath and everything" (Acts 17:24–25).

That's humbling. People (and nations) like to think that we matter, we contribute, we are needed. Nations have massive collective egos, considering themselves important, the last best hope for mankind, God's answer to all that's wrong in the world.

But God has never asked any nation, "How could I have fulfilled my plan without you?" Instead he asks, "What do you have that I need? What can you possibly contribute that I don't already have, or can't do without? Not one thing."

Whatever each nation's political system and power may be, it will soon collapse. And God's purposes will go on invincibly without it. Let all who boast of their nation's greatness (or dread its impending demise), take a deep breath. Every nation shall fail, and God alone will prevail.

All this comforts me in our meltdown world. I admit that corrupt political powers can be terrifying; and that watching your nation give itself over to sin and abuses of power is grieving and alarming. I admit that when nations deny basic rights to their citizens, the outcome is frightening.

But what will happen when God's purpose for all nations is complete? He will throw them all onto the useless trash heap of history.

And the Church, the only nation that matters, the only true nation, the only really Christian nation, the only kingdom-nation God truly loves, will go on forever and ever (Matt. 16:18; 1 Pet. 2:9–10; Rev. 11:15–18).

The Nations Are Less than Nothing Compared to God's Existence

All the nations are as nothing before him,
> *they are accounted by him as less than nothing and*
> *emptiness.*

Isaiah 40:17

When God actually assesses the nations, and measures their virtue and value, they weigh "nothing" and are "less than nothing."

As God continues to comfort his people (Isa. 40:1) he mocks the nations, dispelling the myth of power that they claim. And his rebuke gets stingingly sarcastic at this point. You might even say that he starts trash-talking.

In my observation there are three types of trash talking. First is the abhorrent degrading foul-mouthed flaunting and taunting in which today's male and female athletes seem to revel. Ugly.

Then there is the always-in-good-fun-back-and-forth-banter that goes with the game: "We're not scared of you. This game's ours. You can't stop us because you're nothing, and you've got nothing! Wink. Wink." Pretty insulting—but with a knowing smile of mutual understanding—there's no harm done.

Then there is holy trash talking, which probably only God can pull off (without sinning in the process)—"All the nations are as nothing before him, they are accounted by him as less than nothing and emptiness" (Isa. 40:17). This is God saying to the nations, "You're nothing!"

That's pretty harsh. Nothing means *nothing.* No. Thing. Not. A. Thing.

To be nothing is not good. And if there is something "less than nothing," that would mean that it's not really something or anything, at all. It's sub-nothing. And apparently nations qualify.

Isaiah 40:17 is a holy insult. Compared to God, the nations are less than nothing. God scorns the nations, saying to Babylon, America, Israel, the Arab world, China, and every single nation there is or ever has been: "Apart from my common grace and sovereign plans, you've got nothing! You are nothing! In fact, you're less than nothing—you're absolute utter emptiness!"

Is it even possible to be that insignificant? Apparently it is, for "Those of low estate are but a breath; those of high estate are a delusion; in the balances they go up; they are *together* lighter than a breath" (Ps. 62:9).

Yet, what a lot of noise they make! "Ah, the roar of nations; they roar like the roaring of mighty waters! The nations roar like the roaring of many waters, but he will rebuke them, and they will flee far away, chased like chaff on the mountains before the wind and whirling dust before the storm" (Isa. 17:12–13).

Some have said that "empty trucks make the most noise." And it's true, both on bumpy roads, and in corridors of power. Whether on a pot-holed street or in a power-grabbing Washington, Beijing, Tehran, or Babylon, the nations never stop making noise: "Why do the nations rage and the peoples plot in vain? The kings of the earth set themselves, and the rulers take counsel together, against the LORD and against his Anointed, saying, 'Let us burst their bonds apart and cast away their cords from us'" (Ps. 2:1–3). But these are empty trucks.

God laughs when nations mock. "He who sits in the heavens laughs; the LORD holds them in derision" (Ps. 2:1–4). The nations are so insignificant before God, that he considers them a joke.

I need to find comfort here, or I'll be among those in a panic over the state of today's world. I need to know that all of God's screaming and scheming enemies are nothing but a fleet of empty trucks. Nations think they have power. But they are less than nothing compared to the living God. So when they fuss and fume or mock and malign—I don't need to be afraid. God above is for us below.

This doesn't mean that evil powers will never be able to harm or torment us. I'm afraid they will. Throughout history and all over the world today, nations have hated and harassed believers, and there is no reason to think it won't happen to us.

But what this does mean is that God knows the end of all things; and he mocks those who think they know otherwise. There is nothing that any nation can do to us unless God allows and overrules it for his good purposes.

Certainly this is hard to accept. Don't I know it! But with God's enabling grace, I must and I will stand on this impregnable rock in these troubling times.

Stop Liking to Think of God As . . .

To whom then will you liken God,
    or what likeness compare with him?
An idol! A craftsman casts it,
    and a goldsmith overlays it with gold
    and casts for it silver chains.

Isaiah 40:18–19

Here God comforts Israel by asking a question that accents the obvious: no gods of our own making can compare to him. This was Israel's sin while in her sorrows. Like most humans, she chose imitation pretender-gods for comfort or deliverance, rather than the true and immortal Creator (see also Isa. 37:18–19; 41:29; 42:17; 44:9–20; Rom. 1:22–23; 1 Tim. 1:17; 6:15–16; 1 John 5:21).

But nobody gets to be God other than the One who is God. It is vanity to trust in gods who are not God. Idolatry is simultaneously the greatest evil and the deepest folly of the human heart. It is the arrogance of rebels and the refuge of fools.

I Like to Think of God As . . .

And yet today's world has turned idolatry into a virtue, as is clear from the ever-popular mantra intoned by people everywhere: "I like to think of God as . . ."

Think about the audacity (and futility) of it all. I have. But in a way, I get it. One of the temptations in being seriously ill, like I am, is that it makes me want God to be what I want him to be. I want him to be always safe, always compliant with my wishes, always explaining himself to me, always grandfather-like, always an instantaneous healer, always a right-now deliverer, always a close and cozy friend, always somebody that will make me happy, and always predictable and tame. I wouldn't mind if God were my therapist, grandpa, genie, confidant, teddy bear, and cheerleader—all wrapped into one cuddly package.

But that isn't God!

"I like to think of God as . . ." is the pop-spirituality womb in which idols are conceived. An idol is simply an image representing what someone prefers God to be. It's God created by man rather than the reverse. Or rather, it is seven billion gods, all generated by the "idol factory" in each human heart.

God's point in Isaiah 40 is that idolatry promises what it cannot deliver. The people of Israel felt no real comfort because in that moment they had no real God. They'd exchanged the immortal God for images made of hands (Rom. 1:23). And disappointed grief is the outcome when we do that.

Non-Gods Are No Help

I cannot face a hard life with an imitation god. If I try, I'll be on my own in a cruel and comfortless world, because false gods simply cannot help. How can they—since they only exist in my imagination?

The fortune cookie that reads: "I cannot help you for I am just a cookie" is profound. Idols are equally inept, for they are figments of the imagination; mere chiseled stones, carved logs, molten and molded metal. When people turn to a false god for help they are in fact turning to *nothing* for help. Non-gods are not really there. They have no real existence (1 Cor. 8:4–6). And since they do not exist, they cannot hear or see or deliver (Ps. 115:3–9). So in the end idolaters are helplessly and hopelessly abandoned.

It's true that God is unpredictable. Even though he's in control, sad and bad things happen under his watch. Kids rebel. Churches fail. Nutrition fanatics still die at 40. Healthy-eating kids still get lymphoma. Disasters strike. Cancer and bone disease cut life, ministry and plans short. And nations still defy God and go to war.

This is the hard truth I need to embrace. I need to understand that God can't be understood. I need a category for a God who doesn't fit into my categories. I need to be comfortable with a God who makes me uncomfortable; a God who may well *intentionally* befuddle me, so that I'll walk by faith not by understanding; by faith, not by sight; by faith, not by my opinion of what God should do next.

Difficult as it may be, forsaking our idols and being still to know the true God—and then letting him be the God that he is—is the only comfort and peace we can ever know, whether in life, or in death (Ps. 46:1–11).

Choosing Our God Wisely

He who is too impoverished for an offering
  chooses wood that will not rot;
he seeks out a skillful craftsman
  to set up an idol that will not move.

Isaiah 40:20

God's aim throughout this chapter is to comfort his ancient people (Isa. 40:1–2). He does that here by setting up a contrast and a choice:

You and I can have *either* an idol made of wood that will neither rot, nor move (Isa. 40:20), or we can have "the One who sits enthroned above the circle of the earth, [whose] inhabitants are like grasshoppers" (Isa. 40:22).

We can have idols who are "like scarecrows in a cucumber field, [which] cannot speak [and] have to be carried, for they cannot walk" (Jer. 10:5), or we can have "the King of the ages, immortal, invisible, the only God, [to whom] be honor and glory forever and ever. Amen" (1 Tim. 1:17).

We can have the "futile thinking" and "foolish hearts" that

have "exchanged the glory of the immortal God for images resembling mortal man and birds and animals and creeping things" (Rom. 1:18–23), or we can have "[The] blessed and only Sovereign, the King of kings and Lord of lords, who alone has immortality, who dwells in unapproachable light, whom no one has ever seen or can see. To him be honor and eternal dominion. Amen" (1 Tim. 6:15–16).

Our level of comfort and strength will depend on which option we choose. So what will it be?

Before we decide we should notice a couple of (I think intended) sarcastic ironies in God's words here in Isaiah 40:20.

First, God describes the one who "chooses wood that *will not rot.*" Note God's sarcasm. The man is concerned that his god might rot, so he chooses really hard wood. But that is the best his idol can do: "not rot." It is utterly lifeless, of course, being a long-dead tree limb—but at least it won't decompose! (For more of God's sarcastic irony, see Isaiah 44:9–20.)

Next, the idolator sets up "an idol that will not move." In his effort to create an immovable idol that he can depend on to be there, he hammers and nails it into place; thereby setting up an idol that is unable to move at all; one that cannot be anywhere but where it is—unless it is carried (Jer. 10:3–5).

But gods that cannot move don't do us much good when we are somewhere else in all the various comings and goings of life. Which is better—to have a dead god which never rots, or a living God who never dies? Which is the better, more comforting choice—a god who cannot move, or a God who is always on the move; who is everywhere, all the time, and all at once?

Besides: "Their idols are silver and gold, the work of human hands. They have mouths, but do not speak; eyes, but do not see. They have ears, but do not hear; noses, but do not smell. They have hands, but do not feel; feet, but do not walk; and they do not make a sound in their throat. *Those who make them become like them; so do all who trust in them* (Ps. 115:3–8; 135:18).

What people devote their attention and affection to, is what they become. Which makes devotion to a piece of mute, blind, deaf, unfeeling, and immobile piece of wood or stone a pretty risky commitment after all.

The point of this is not to mock others' faith, as if we are better than them. We're not. We've all been idolators with gods—people, possessions, power, politics, or plans—that we have loved more than God; substitutes for God which we've trusted for our ultimate security or happiness. The point isn't to mock false gods like God does; but to show that it matters that we choose our god or God wisely.

In Isaiah 40:20, God wants us to know that we can choose a god who cannot see, hear, think or feel—a god we have to crowbar loose and carry around because its been nailed in place. Or we can choose a God who carries us; one who lives and moves and sees and hears and acts and speaks and comforts. One who will be there and here, with unfailing love, for all eternity!

Inexcusable Ignorance

Do you not know? Do you not hear?
  Has it not been told you from the beginning?
  Have you not understood from the foundations of the
    earth?

Isaiah 40:21

With these words, the prophet introduces what he is about to say in Isaiah 40:22: that God sits as king over all the earth with a bunch of tiny human grasshoppers living here below—and he implies strongly that they should have known this, and should never have doubted it for a moment.

To feel this stinging rebuke we could paraphrase it like this: "How do you not know? How have you not heard? Haven't you been told this from the beginning of time? And how is it that you do not understand what has been revealed since the foundation of the earth? It is he—God—who sits above the circle of the earth."

The ancient Israelites are scolded because there were things about God that they should and could have known; but didn't. Since they should have known better, they were inexcusably ignorant.

But how could they have known about God "from the beginning" of time and "from the foundation of the earth?" What was it that happened "in the beginning" that "told" them about God so that they "understood" the truth about him (or at least should have)?

Creation is what happened (Gen. 1:1). From the beginning of time when God laid the foundation of the world, his creation has been telling everybody about the living Creator-God. Throughout all the ages Creation has been the voice of God, speaking through all the things that he has made.

> Psalm 19:1–4a, "The heavens declare the glory of God, and the sky above proclaims his handiwork. Day to day pours out speech, and night to night reveals knowledge. There is no speech, nor are there words, whose voice is not heard. Their voice [that is, the voice of the heavens and sun] goes out through all the earth, and their words to the end of the world" (see also Rom. 10:18).

> Acts 14:15b–17, "[W]e bring you good news, that you should turn from these vain things to a living God, who made the heaven and the earth and the sea and all that is in them. In past generations he allowed all the nations to walk in their own ways. Yet he did not leave himself without witness, for he did good by giving you rains from heaven and fruitful seasons, satisfying your hearts with food and gladness."

> Romans 1:19–20, "For what can be known about God is

plain to them, because God has shown it to them. For his invisible attributes, namely, his eternal power and divine nature, have been clearly perceived, ever since the creation of the world, in the things that have been made. So they are without excuse."

The fact that a finite cosmos exists proves that an infinite, self-sustaining Creator exists. If once the world did not exist, and now it does, then Someone or something that pre-exists and self-exists had to bring the world into being. Creation proves the existence and proclaims the attributes of God.

Just like the God revealed in Scripture is full of wisdom, power, goodness, faithfulness, mercy, love, wrath, and judgment; so, too, the God revealed in Nature is full of wisdom, power, goodness, faithfulness, mercy, love, wrath, and judgment. Scripture and nature are God talking to us all the time. And he's been telling us who he is and what he's like from the beginning of time and the foundation of the earth. That's why God asks, "How is it that you don't know and understand?"

This is what keeps me believing and hoping. God's Word and his world tell me that God is, and that he is strong, wise, and good enough to make all things. And that being so, I can know that he is strong, wise, and good enough to take care of me, whatever may come my way.

O Lord God above, please don't let me ever hear you say, "Tim, How did you not know? How could you not understand about my existence and character, even though I showed them to you every single day?" Father God, please give me ears to receive, eyes to see, a mind to understand, and a will to surrender, as I hear your voice through your word and world every single day of my life.

God Above and Us Below

It is he who sits above the circle of the earth,
*   and its inhabitants are like grasshoppers;*
who stretches out the heavens like a curtain,
*   and spreads them like a tent to dwell in;*

Isaiah 40:22

Behold the supremacy of God. God is above and we are below. He sits enthroned over all that is, and we humans are as grasshoppers before him. Behold: this is God in his place, and us in ours.

This verse and I go way back to the early 80s (in my mid-twenties), when I summarized this chapter and verse like this: "There is one true God who owns a place of supreme dominion over all people, destinies, nations, and creation, by which he irresistibly governs the universe, personally sustains all things, and freely and perfectly accomplishes his will; to the end that glory might crown his name and good might come to his people."

Each part of that is at least hinted at in Isaiah 40.

Then in the early 2000s (in my mid-forties), I had an early morning encounter with God. Like countless mornings, I had started my quiet time with this prayer: "Dear Father, please help me to see your glory in your Word this morning so I can become more in love with you, and in awe of you, than I am now."

God loves to answer such a prayer, and he did that morning, once again with Isaiah 40:22 as the inspiration. That's when God came into view, and joy surged as my pen tried to keep pace. Here's what I received and wrote:

> God is the God who sits enthroned above all things, whose hands are never tired; whose eyes are never shut; whose will is never frustrated; whose plans are never scrapped; whose love is never quenched; whose promises are never broken; whose mercies are never old; whose help is never late; whose power is never taxed; whose mind is never surprised; whose throne is never threatened; whose knowledge is never increased; whose being is never altered;

> Whose decrees, decisions, and judgments are never revoked; whose Word has never failed; whose Truth has never faltered; whose ways can never be predicted; whose paths can never be traced; whose depths can never be fathomed; whose mystery can never be plumbed; whose ultimate ends can never ever be foiled.

> He is the one in whose ocean of sovereignty no power of heaven, or demon of hell, or scheme of rulers, or deep, dark, sinful choice of man can create even the tiniest

ripple. He that sits in the heavens laughs at hell's schemes, Satan's plans, man's rebellions, and sin's worst.

Before God everything is but an insect. And nothing seems nearly so big or threatening or important or ominous when placed beside him. He stands astride the universe, with one foot firmly planted in the east and another in the west, and his arms gather the galaxies in their embrace. As vast as it all is, his immensity surpasses it all.

That was in my forties. And now in my mid-sixties—while fighting for my life—I'm back for more of him. As I contend for faith, hope, and joy, I've returned to where I was way back then: contemplating Isaiah's Supreme Being, the true and living God, all over again.

But there is some sadness. They say that at least half of all humans claim to believe in a "supreme being." But those words don't seem to mean what people think they mean, since so few who believe in a Supreme Being actually seek, serve, and love him *supremely*. How tragic that the Supreme Being gets little more than the table scraps of human time, thought, affection, or love.

When I search for "supreme" here's what I see: "superior to all others, paramount, sovereign, topmost, utmost, highest." So "Supreme Being" is a very worthy title for God, for God is by definition, all that.

But for most, something's been lost in translation, so that while many say they believe in a *supreme* being, they actually give him no more than an apathetic shrug and indifferent yawn?

May it never be true of me. Instead, may I truly see God enthroned supreme, far above the cosmos; so immense that he outstretches his arms to open the heavens like we would open a curtain; and to expand the skies overhead as if he were pitching a tent to cover us.

O God, you are my God.

Early will I seek you,

And all the day long.

The Nations Can Do Nothing without God's Existence

Who brings princes to nothing,
  and makes the rulers of the earth as emptiness.
Scarcely are they planted, scarcely sown,
  scarcely has their stem taken root in the earth,
when he blows on them, and they wither,
  and the tempest carries them off like stubble.

Isaiah 40:23–24

It intrigues me how much God talks about the nations while seeking to comfort us. Apparently, right thinking about the nations is comforting for those living among them.

And it remains so for us today. I saw that yesterday's news headlined at least ten war zones on planet earth, and that is only a fraction of the armed tribal, national, and international conflicts raging over who is going to rule whom and where.

So how does God respond to the morning news? With four assertions that I've made more personal than earlier; made more personal because God takes these things personally:

- The Nations Matter Nothing to Me (Isa. 40:15)
- The Nations Contribute Nothing to Me (Isa. 40:16)
- The Nations Are Less Than Nothing Compared to Me (Isa. 40:17)
- The Nations Can Be and Do Nothing without Me (Isa. 40:23–24)

I believe hard days loom before us. If the nations hated our Master, they will hate us, too. But Isaiah 40 is meant to inform us how to respond to the hatred and headlines. According to God, every ruler is "emptiness" and will be "brought to nothing." Whether powerful tyrants coveting world domination, or tin-pot drug lords expanding their turf, they rise and fall by an act of God. He speaks, and "Presto!" they are there. Then he blows, and "Poof!" they are gone.

How comforting to any of us who are needlessly fired up or frantic in this this election season. What Isaiah is saying is that it is God who deposes one ruler and installs another. Rulers are mere pawns; which means I can chill. Today's text tells me that campaigns don't produce candidates. Votes don't decide presidents. Politicking doesn't win elections. Conspiracies don't affect outcomes. Coups don't determine kings. Overthrows don't topple dictators. Power doesn't take thrones. Invasions don't draw boundaries (Acts 17:26).

God sets rulers in place and he blows them down. Nations do not exist apart from his will and cannot rule without his permission. I don't pretend to know all the reasons, but biblical history suggests that if, in God's mind, a nation needs to be humbled, God will set up a ruler who will do stupid things. If a nation needs blessing, God will install someone wise. If a nation deserves to be punished, God will seat someone in power who will blunder them into a bloody war or economic collapse.

If a nation enslaves humans, practices injustice, or kills unborn babies, God will make them pay. If a nation needs peace, he will give them a peacemaker. If a nation is puffed with pride, he will install a ruler who will make a fool of them. If a nation is self-righteous he will enthrone a ruler who will expose or embody their hidden national sins. If a nation needs a chance to hear the gospel, he will put rulers in place who—through our prayers—will intentionally or otherwise establish peace and quiet so the gospel may advance to all people (1 Tim. 2:1–5).

Rulers are not chosen by vote, might, or coup; they are chosen by God to give a nation exactly what it deserves (under God's judgment), or needs (according to his mercies). That's how it works. Which means that you and I may well go ahead and vote if and how we choose. But then we'd do well to take a deep breath, leave it all in the hands of God, and not worry about how it turns out. That is God's concern, not ours.

And yes, I know—at least in part—how ugly and scary it can all get. All nations (except God's consecrated nation, the Church, 1 Pet. 2:9, 10) really are godless to one degree or another. And it's only a matter of time before they come to get us believers like they have Israel in olden times, and the Church throughout the ages. But they are wind-blown stubble. And soon, yes, very soon, he who is the Lord of the nations will come, and blow them all into oblivion (Rev. 11:15; 15:3–4).

In the meanwhile, ours is simply to pray for our leaders, to be godly, and to walk humbly, justly, respectfully, and gently, no matter who's in power, or what evil they may inflict upon us (Micah 6:8; Col. 4:5–6; 1 Tim. 2:1–5; 1 Pet. 2:9–17; 3:13–17).

Day Twenty-Three

The Incomparable God

To whom then will you compare me,
that I should be like him? says the Holy One.

Isaiah 40:25

I'm besieged with pain again. In cahoots with my aching back, hips, hands, and jaw, the stabbing knife of my 35-year headache is twisting misery into my head. How many mornings in a row is this?

But I want to rise above my pain by considering the incomparability of God; the focus of today's Isaiah 40:25 text.

I notice first that the Questioner in this verse is called "The Holy One." That is not just a description of God's sinlessness; it is also an affirmation of his "otherness." The word "holy" means separate, different, other, distinct. This is a title describing the utter uniqueness of God. He is the Holy, Holy, Holy One whose glory fills the whole earth (Isa. 6:3).

There is no one like the Holy One to whom he can be compared. This is because in his essence, he is profoundly different than all others. He is a Being in an Order of one. There isn't any other of his kind.

For this reason, to compare others to God and God to others is the ultimate "apples-to-oranges" futility. You just cannot do it.

On the one hand, the God of Isaiah 40 is a comforting, glorious, trustworthy, and Mighty Ruler, who is the all-wise, all-good, and ever-awake Creator, who is a Lord of the nations, Shepherd of the sheep, keeper of the stars, and the never-tired Creator who gives power to the weary and wings to the fallen.

And on the other hand, all other gods are engraved stones and logs; figments of human imagination, carved into pieces of wood. And even we humans, image-bearers of God though we are, are still but mere creatures.

There simply is no comparison between him and us, or anything else in all creation.

I think there's a subtle nuance in how the question is asked that is meant to illuminate just how *other* and *different* God is. Think about it: the Holy One asks who there is for him to "*be like*," which is to imply that he is not like anyone, even though, in some infinitesimal ways, we are like him.

To be like someone is not the same as being someone that others are like.

The point of God's question is not just that nobody is fully like God, but that God is not really like anyone. God is the Original; everyone and everything else are but poor-quality copies of him. The pool is deep here, but it's worth the plunge.

When making comparisons, we don't normally compare the greater to the lesser but the lesser to the greater.

Simone Biles is the greater; she isn't like anyone in what she does. Some are a little bit like Simone Biles, but in the gymnastics world, she is the unmatched and unmatchable one to which everyone and everything else is compared.

Larry Bird's shot was not like Tim Shorey's. Tim Shorey's shot was in the slightest most shadowy and rare kind of way like Larry Bird's.

The ocean is not like a puddle. The puddle is in the smallest sense, a bit like the ocean.

The sun is not like a 40-watt bulb. A 40-watt bulb is in the tiniest sense a bit like the sun.

Niagara Falls is not like an open faucet. An open faucet is in a minuscule sense like Niagara.

Even so: God isn't like anyone; even if, in some small ways, we're like him. Which means, I think, that God is mocking all comparisons between him and anyone.

The incomparable otherness of God is why, while I've grieved and lamented my circumstances, I have never been angry with God, or shaken my fist at his decrees, or questioned his wisdom. He simply functions so far above and beyond me that I'll never fathom him. And so, he is to be trusted even when he is not understood (Isa. 55:8–11).

This can be so hard. God is so mysterious in his incomparability, that we have to accept *not knowing* as a way of faith and life. However, if we don't accept *not knowing*, we will be restless and angry fist-shakers for all our days.

But if we accept the simple premise that he is there in all of his matchless glory, goodness, wisdom, and power, we will "go out in joy and be led forth in peace" (Isa. 55:12); even while we weep.

The God Who Counts and Cares

Lift up your eyes on high and see:
  who created these?
He who brings out their host by number,
  calling them all by name;
by the greatness of his might
  and because he is strong in power,
  not one is missing.

Isaiah 40:26

I'm feeling a deep sigh of comfort here, and I need to let it sink in.

A skeptic once asked me why God would create as much wasted space with no "practical" purpose as there is in the cosmos. He thought that the vast reaches of what seems to be pointlessly uninhabited space argued against the existence of an all-knowing and all-wise God.

In response, I would never concede that there is any wasted space without any "practical" purpose. How could we possibly know the intricacies of God's design? And besides: let's define "practical." If something is "practical" it is useful and serves a purpose. So if something exists in order to make humans go "Wow!" with overflowing joy (which is what the vastness of space does), is that not a practical purpose?

What if (and there is no "if" about it) there are more than 300-billion (that's 300,000,000,000) galaxies made up of more than 200 sextillion stars (that's 2,000,000,000,000,000,

000,000, if I have my zeroes right, which I doubt) with a vast expanse between every one of them, simply because it takes all of that to shine forth the resplendent majesty of God?

What if the vast immensity of the star-emblazoned universe all exists to shout "Glory!" (Ps. 29:1, 2, 9); to make us go "Wow!" and then bow in joyful adoring awe before the One who spoke each blazing ball of fire into being. After all, the heavens are meant to declare the glory of God, and if the galaxies don't do that, what does (Ps. 19:1ff)?

Now as for the stars, "[God] brings out their host by number, calling them all by name; [and] by the greatness of his might and because he is strong in power, not one is missing (see also Ps. 147:4).

He has them numbered. He has them named. And he has them safe.

For the record, the stars aren't the only things that God numbers and/or names:

- Every measure of dust (Isa. 40:12, "He has enclosed the dust of earth in a measure.")
- Every gallon in the sea (Isa. 40:12, "He has measured the waters in the hollow of his hand.")

- The number of our days and months (Job 14:5, "Man's days are determined, and the number of his months is with you.")

- All our steps (Job 31:4, "Does he not see my ways and number all my steps?")

- What the wind weighs (Job 28:25, "He gave to the word its weight and apportioned the waters by measure.")

- The clouds (Job 38:37, "Who [except God] can number the clouds?")

- When the pregnant doe is due (Job 39:2, "Can you [like God] number the months, and do you know the time until a doe gives birth?")

- How often I toss in bed at night (Ps. 56:8, "You have kept count of my tossings and put my tears in a bottle.")

- The days I will live (Ps. 139:16, "In your book were written, every one of them, the days that were formed for me, when as yet there were none of them.")

- Each falling bird (Matt 10:29, "Not one of them will fall to the ground apart from your Father.")

- The hairs on my head (Matt 10:30, "But even the hairs of your head are all numbered.")

- All of his sheep (John 10:3, 28, "He calls his own sheep by name," and, Jesus says, "no one will snatch them out of my hand.")

Like with the stars, God has us numbered. He has us named. He has us safe.

He calls us all by number. He gives us each a name. And

because he is strong in power not one of us is missing (either in this life or in the next).

Herein is God's all-knowing specific and detailed attentiveness (he's numbered us all).

Herein is his personal love (he has given us a name, and unlike me with everybody, he remembers it). And herein is eternal safety and security (because he is strong, not one of us is missing).

If he does all this for the stars, he will do it for us—which is, after all, Isaiah 40's whole point.

Feeling Unseen and Unheard

Why do you say, O Jacob,
*   and speak, O Israel,*
*"My way is hidden from the L*ORD*,*
*   and my right is disregarded by my God"?*

Isaiah 40:27

It's sad, but having just said that he is the incomparable God who numbers, names, and keeps all the stars, and by implication, all of us, God now has to gently rebuke his people for their reaction to their current sorrows. Because they felt like their plight was unseen (i.e., "hidden from the LORD") and their rights were unheard (i.e., "disregarded" by their God), they were charging God on two counts: lack of attentive care and failure to be just.

Let me be clear. Most of the time, there is no sin in *feeling* unseen and unheard; the many laments and "How long" groanings in the Bible validate such emotions. In fact, what else can we do but groan, and ask "How Long" and "Why" when God's plan for our life offers so much grief and so few answers. But the ancient Israelites weren't just *feeling* this; they were *say*ing it and *speak*ing it. And apparently they crossed a line in how they were venting it all.

God's response is a warning to us. The issue here is not their grief or even their painful confusion and doubts. Remember that God has already validated their grief by offering comfort for it (Isa. 40:1–2). God is not a cold-hearted emotional sadist who permits all kinds of tears in our lives without any compassion. He cares when we hurt.

Take yesterday for example. A twelve-hour sneezing, nose-blowing, and overall head-cold-like misery (of mysterious origin and seemingly random purpose) piled onto my miserable pre-existing conditions, and had me fighting back tears more than once.

I don't think that God was upset with my pain-filled tears, or those moments when I sincerely wondered "Why?" But if I had said to God, "You're not seeing me, hearing me, or treating me fairly. You're being unjust. And by the way, while I've got your ear, you've been treating me like that for a long time." I'm quite sure the Hoy Spirit would have talked to me about my sinful accusations against God.

The point is that it's not okay for me to impugn the justice of God. I need to be very careful with God. Yes, I can honestly express my griefs, pour out my longings, vent my "How longs?" and even tell God that I am *feeling* abandoned or mistreated by him (e.g., Psalm 13). But I must be careful not to accuse God of doing wrong, like Israel did.

I think that sometimes, in our efforts to help people be

honest with God, we almost imply that anything goes with God; like we have a right, not only to weep and ask why, but also to put God on trial as if he answers to us.

But God's point in today's text is not to scold Israel so much as to assure them of the very thing they were doubting. True, it is a mild rebuke, and one worth heeding. But God's point is not to rebuke. His point (in Isa. 40:26–27) is to say to his people, "No, your way is not hidden from me. And no, I am not disregarding your rights and needs. Remember that I am the one who has made, numbered, named, and kept the stars—and since I do that for the stars, you can be sure that I will always and unfailingly do that for you!"

I must be careful not to accuse God of wrongdoing; it matters that I revere him enough, not to do that. But I also need to know that he loves and cares for me. I am not hidden from his sight, and never ever will be. Likewise, he has never disregarded my rights and needs. Rather, he has so seen my plight and regarded my circumstances that he has sent his Son to be the loving Savior and Deliverer I so desperately need.

In fact, if I ever am feeling unseen, unheard, and disregarded by God, the best remedy is to remember in the words of the hymn, that "Christ has regarded my helpless estate, and has shed his own blood for my soul" (Horatio Spafford, "It Is Well with My Soul").

What more could he say or do to convince me of his love?

Day Twenty-Six

The Everlasting God, Our Creator

Have you not known? Have you not heard?
The LORD is the everlasting God,
   the Creator of the ends of the earth.

Isaiah 40:28a

Once again, God speaks through his prophet to ask his doubting people, "Why are you murmuring against me (Isa. 40:27)? Haven't you known the truth? And haven't you heard what I've been saying?" Given how God had spoken through nature, Scripture, and prophecies, they certainly should have heard and known the truth, but they had forgotten it, or never really heard it at all.

Israel suffered with spiritual deafness and amnesia. Just like those who have had a traumatic head injury or other catastrophic event often experience amnesia, forgetting who they are and what's happened to them, Israel had been traumatized by many sorrows, making them deaf and forgetful.

I know the condition well. In fact it's one reason I've kept a daily journal (including this 31-day journey through Isaiah 40) during my prolonged cancer and bone disease trials. And it's why I keep writing about truths I already know: because I've been traumatized by sorrows, becoming prone to deafness and amnesia just like everyone else can be. As troubles mount up, hearing impairment and forgetfulness can set in, and I've had to fight to keep hearing and remembering what God has said.

Yet in Isaiah 40, God doesn't want to scold so much as comfort; this time with two resounding assertions that should thunder from the high heavens.

But first, I want to note what God is in view here. He is the LORD, with all capital letters. Whenever there's a fully capitalized Bible reference to the LORD, the translators are referencing one specific God, whose Hebrew name is Yahweh; the God of the Bible. This isn't just a reference to a vague and nebulous deity; a casual nod to God in the abstract. Instead it's a bold assertion that the LORD (Yahweh) is the only true God. For of all the gods there are, he alone is the Everlasting God and Almighty Creator—never to be confused with a world that's full of pretenders.

Here now are Isaiah's two thunderous declarations about Yahweh, the God of the Bible: (1) Yahweh is the everlasting God, and (2) Yahweh is the Creator of all that is. And here I stand: my whole life and faith rest on these pillars. Take them away and whoever and whatever Tim Shorey is, comes crashing down.

The One who is everlasting, without beginning or end is the Creator who gave a beginning to all else that exists. Yahweh is the origin of all things while having no origin. He "inhabits eternity" (Isa. 57:15) as the only independent and self-sufficient One who has existence, being, and life in himself. And he is the source from whom all other beings and objects derive their existence (Acts 17:24–28).

He is the everlasting "I AM," the Unmoved Mover, the Beginner without a beginning, and the Uncreated Creator. He is always ancient, but never old. Like Moses' bush, God is always a flaming fire that needs no fuel, and always ablaze with scorching heat, but never giving off so much as a whiff of smoke. He is the everlasting God and the Creator of all (Exod. 3:2, 14; Dan. 7:9; Heb. 11:3).

As the psalmist puts it, "LORD, you have been our dwelling place in all generations. Before the mountains were brought forth, or ever you had formed the earth and the world, from everlasting to everlasting you are God" (Ps. 90:1–2).

And again, "The eternal God is your dwelling place, and underneath are the everlasting arms" (Deut. 33:27).

And again, "Your throne is established from of old; you are from everlasting" (Ps. 93:2).

And again, "You keep him in perfect peace whose mind is stayed on you, because he trusts in you. Trust in the LORD forever, for the LORD God is an everlasting rock" (Isa. 26:3–4).

And again, "But the LORD is the true God; he is the living God and everlasting King" (Jer. 10:10a).

The God of Isaiah 40, the everlasting God and Almighty Creator who comforted in Isaiah's day is alive and comforting today. For he is "the blessed and only Sovereign, the King of kings and Lord of lords, who alone has immortality, who dwells in unapproachable light, whom no one has ever seen [i.e., in his full blazing glory] or can see. To him be honor and eternal dominion. Amen" (1 Tim. 6:15–16).

Amen, indeed. Let us trust in him forever.

The God Who Never Sleeps

> *He does not faint or grow weary;*
> *his understanding is unsearchable.*
>
> Isaiah 40:28b

This is an interesting combination of statements about God; not a connection we'd naturally expect. God doesn't faint or sleep, and, by the way, he *does* understand everything. What's the connection? Somehow, God's indefatigable strength relates to his unsearchable understanding, which results in our comfort, which is the whole point of Isaiah 40. But how? How does God's never getting tired or sleeping relate to God knowing everything and us being comforted? I think I know.

My senior year of college was doubtlessly my busiest ever. I was married with a child. I also worked 20–25 hours per week on a 3:00–8:00 am UPS graveyard shift. Plus I had 22 credit hours of courses. Plus I played on the college basketball team. Plus I/we had several friendships we were actively cultivating.

Something had to give. And sleep was it. I "fueled" all these extracurriculars with a mere three to four hours sleep per night, and whatever other sleep I could catch between and during classes. In fact, my biology professors let me sleep through their classes so long as I passed the course.

I learned two things from the experience. First, I was not built for such madness. In fact, I had to stop playing ball with a couple weeks left in the season because my body gave out. Severe exhaustion with profuse night sweats warned me to stop. Moral of the story? Tim, you do not have a boundless supply of energy. You need rest and replenishment. Lesson learned.

There's a reason why Gayline's and my first question of the morning is, "How did you sleep?" We ask this first-of-the-morning question because nighttime sleep can indicate how our daytime will go. Most of us humans need seven or eight hours sleep per night to get replenished. God alone needs no plug or battery-pack to re-energize. All the rest of us come with a re-charging cord called "sleep."

Secondly, because I grew tired and weary—and fell asleep often—if affected my knowledge and understanding. My grades suffered, and my thinking and reasoning powers were depleted significantly. You can't learn anything, or know what's going on, or understand what needs to be understood, or reason clearly when your brain and body are sunk in utter exhaustion. We humans need sleep. But when we are asleep we're not knowing or understanding what's going on around us. We need sleep to replenish strength and to think, know, and understand. But we can't think, know, and understand while we're sleeping.

Thankfully, God is not like us. He never gets tired or needs to sleep, and so he knows and understands everything that's happening, all the time and everywhere. When I get up from a nap, I often ask Gayline, "Is there any news?" In other words, "What happened in the world or in our tiny little corner of it, while I was sleeping? Did I miss anything?"

Those are questions God never asks, because God never takes a nap. He never wakes up and asks if there is any news, because he never goes to sleep in the first place. God's understanding of all that is going on in his world and in our lives is constant, comprehensive, and unsearchable because he is always awake and on watch to see it happen.

What sweet comfort this is for God's people! What comfort there is in knowing that God never dozes off while on watch; nor does he ever sleep through our sorrows and sufferings. He's always awake, always alert, always aware, and always attuned to our circumstances with a complete understanding of everything that is going on in every single one of our lives.

But as for me, I am now bone-weary and have occasional night sweats for far different reasons. Cancer, a stubborn bone-infection, relentless pain, and various treatments and meds make me incessantly exhausted. I am never *not tired*. I can't even remember what "not tired" feels like.

But this I believe: that "he who keeps [me] will not slumber. Behold, he who keeps Israel will neither slumber nor sleep" (Ps. 121:3–4). So as I go to the doctor today for the latest assessment of my bone disease, my Heavenly Father won't be caught napping. Instead, he will meet me there; wide awake, very present, and fully aware to comfort and care.

Exhaustion and Our Vocabulary of Self

He gives power to the faint,
    and to him who has no might he increases strength.
Even youths shall faint and be weary,
    and young men shall fall exhausted;

Isaiah 40:29–30

Yes. I'm exhausted; and I think with fair enough reason. I've said recently that I suffer from CC-LABS; as in C—cancer, C—cranial pain, L—lumbar injuries, A—advancing arthritis, B—bone disease, and S—side effects from all my treatments; all at once, and all for a very long time. And I haven't even mentioned my old age. So, to say that I am weary of it all is to understate it massively.

I can relate to the people in today's text. The "faint" are those weak-kneed and light-headed with fatigue. Those with "no might" are powerless to take another step. The "weary" are worn out and depleted. And the "exhausted" are at the end of themselves; so feeble and emptied out that they stumble and fall. These parallel Hebrew expressions describe a profound lack of strength; a total exhaustion of body and spirit; a feeling like I've often had—as if someone has unplugged me, vacuumed all my insides out, and then left me to die.

The degree of their weariness suggests that these people were not just exhausted; they *knew* they were exhausted. You cannot be this kind of tired and not know it. And tiredness this deep cannot be pushed through. So the idea here is not merely that God keeps his eye out for weary people and lends them a hand when they need it. No. God doesn't help all who are weak and helpless; he helps all *who know and admit* that they are profoundly weak and helpless.

To repeat: this promise is given to a specific group of people, to those who are tired and who clearly know it. They've stopped drawing from their own reservoirs of strength. They know that it is not by their might or power that they survive (Zech. 4:6). They and their resources are exhausted. Their *self-reliance* is depleted. They have nothing left.

Which means that to experience the strength of God I have to renounce my membership in the self-sufficiency club. I dare not be like the rich farmer who self-reliantly felt no need for God because his barns were full. Having my barns filled with self-confidence and reliance might lead to momentary success, but it will ultimately end in disappointment, exhaustion, and ruin (Luke 12:16–21).

This isn't how the world thinks. In fact, the world has created a huge vocabulary of self; hyphenated *self* words that dominate mindsets. Self-help, self-worth, self-image, self-reliance, self-sufficiency, self-confidence, self-assur-ance, self-respect, self-esteem, self-actualization, self-defense, self-expression, self-fulfillment, self-definition, self-determination, self-government. Never in history has such unblushing self-worship been so fashionable. The cult of Self is rampant.

Of course there is a right view of self for the believer. We are made in the image of God, loved by the Father, purchased by the blood of Christ, in-dwelt by the Spirit of God, and des-tined for eternal glory. There's a whole lot of God-bestowed value and honor to be enjoyed there, and we should be grateful for it.

But none of this should lead to the vanity of self-love so prevalent today. A narcissistic view of *self* isn't compatible with Isaiah 40. God doesn't say: "They who wait on themselves or believe in themselves or are sure of themselves shall renew their strength." He says the opposite. Strength does not come to the self-reliant and self-assured; it comes to those who have come to the end of self; to those who despair because their trusted self-resources are gone; to those who know they are the faint, the feeble, and the fallen.

Which includes me. I'm looking at a long exhausting road ahead. Unless God chooses to heal me—which of course he can and might—I will never endure. My "self" is already spent, and I have many long miles to go, likely with years of suffering, pain, and sorrow still ahead.

Out of the depths of my exhaustion I can only wait upon the One who can make me strong. For where self ends, strength begins. And only when "Self's" barns are depleted can God's best be known. O Lord, I confess it: My barns are empty and my cupboards are bare.

The Waiting Room

But they who wait for the LORD shall renew their strength . . .

Isaiah 40:31a

Life is a waiting room. In my experience, there is almost always a delay between the moment we learn of a need, and the time that need is met. And very often that wait is long. Which means that waiting on the Lord is an everyday experience. To be sure, we rarely enjoy waiting. But what today's text (and many others) promise is that good things come to those who willingly wait:

- "I will wait for the LORD . . . and I will hope in him" (Isa. 8:17)
- "It will be said on that day, 'Behold, this is our God; we have waited for him, that he might save us. This is the LORD; we have waited for him; let us be glad and rejoice in his salvation" (Isa. 25:9)
- "You keep him in perfect peace whose mind is stayed on you, because he trusts in you. Trust in the LORD

forever, for the Lord God is an everlasting rock" (Isa. 26:3–4)

- "For thus said the Lord GOD . . .' In returning and rest you shall be saved; in quietness and in trust shall be your strength' . . . Therefore the LORD waits to be gracious to you, and therefore he exalts himself to show mercy to you. For the LORD is a God of justice; blessed are all those who wait for him" (Isa. 30:15a, 18)
- "O LORD, be gracious to us; we wait for you. Be our arm every morning, our salvation in the time of trouble" (Isa, 33:2)

What prayers and promises these are! And what encouragements to wait with grace! But what is true waiting on the Lord?

Trusting Hope

To wait on the Lord is to actively expect the coming blessing of God. It trusts in hope that all God's promises will come to fruition. It says to the weary heart, "Be strong; fear not! Behold, your God will come . . . and save you" (Isa. 35:4). Yes. He will come. He will save. And he will fulfill our deepest longings.

Quiet Rest

"In quietness and trust shall be your strength" (Isa. 30:15). Quietness is the opposite of panicking and pushing. It speaks of peaceful rest; a calm at the storm's center. When mountains tremble, waters roar, nations rage and kingdoms totter, the trusting weary soul remains still, knowing that God is God (Ps. 46:1–11).

Faithful Prayer

"O LORD, in distress they sought you; they poured out a whispered prayer when your discipline was upon them" (Isa. 26:16). Like Hannah of old who longed for a son, those waiting on God will keep talking to God, even if only in a whisper or a groan (1 Sam. 1:12–13; Rom. 8:23). That's me most days. I'm not sure I should admit this, but I'm not into long and loud prayers much anymore. A groaning cry or silent cry or whispered plea is about as good as I can do. But I still pray—as do all who are waiting on the Lord.

Confident Patience

Waiting means delay. God sometimes hides his face, delaying to show his hand. Often he comes with the dawn, but first we have to endure the weeping that lasts for the night (Ps. 30:5; 130:5–6). He has a time-table only his—and we have to be willing to wait in hope of his sure and precious promises.

It's true that God is never late. But it's also true that he is never early or in a hurry. He is always on time, but he is always on his time, and never ahead of time. Grace will come to us precisely when it will do us and others the most good, while simultaneously achieving for God the most glory.

To that end, God will often make us wait; the only question being whether we will wait in confident patience, or complaining impatience. As for me, my waiting list is long. God is making me wait on the removal of my ever-present burdensome medical fanny pack, on the healing of all my diseases, on the salvation of those I love, on the righting of all wrongs, on the return of Jesus, and on the renewal of all things.

We each have our own waiting lists and waiting rooms. Oh for the grace to wait on the Lord until he renews our strength and fulfills all our longings once and for all. Oh that the Morning would dawn!

Measured Strength for Those Who Wait

But they who wait for the LORD shall renew their strength;
*   they shall mount up with wings like eagles;*
they shall run and not be weary;
*   they shall walk and not faint.*

Isaiah 40:31

Here is a haven for every exhausted saint. If we wait upon the Lord in trusting hope, quiet rest, faithful prayer, and confident patience—as considered in the last meditation—then the Lord will renew our strength and keep us from fainting or falling. And he will keep his promise to measure out strength and grace for all the varying circumstances of life.

Measured grace is grace given in keeping with our need in the moment. God never floods us with random grace-overflow or superfluous strength. He doesn't pour into us an ocean of grace when only a cupful is needed; nor does he hand us a tea cup when a flood is the necessary portion.

Like with the widow's flask of oil in Elisha's day, God's oil of strength will flow into us until the need is met, and the vessels are full. God won't let the oil of his provision be carelessly spilled on the ground. Rather, he fills us full enough and just enough, for whatever need we have (2 Kings 4:1–7).

I love John Blanchard's words: "God supplies perfectly measured grace to meet the daily needs of the godly. For daily needs there is daily grace; for sudden needs, sudden grace; for overwhelming needs, overwhelming grace. God's grace is given wonderfully, not wastefully; freely but not foolishly; bountifully but not blindly" (John Blanchard, cited by Jerry Bridges in *Trusting God*).

Deuteronomy 33:25 promises us that "as your days, so shall your strength be," which means that God will strengthen us for whatever each day brings. Likewise, Psalm 84:7 promises that we will "go from strength to strength" (or rampart to rampart) in approaching God, experiencing new strength with each new step.

I see this truth in today's text, where Isaiah identifies three different kinds of strength: strength for running, for soaring, and for walking.

Sometimes we are called to run. These are life moments when our pace is marked by full-speed, calendar-busting, heart-pumping busyness in the building of home and church. And if we wait on the Lord he will meet us in the sprint, and measure out his strength to us.

Other seasons are so sad and heavy that we need transporting grace; times when we can soar on eagle's wings, wings given to us by God to lift us above it all. This is when

God gives grace to be in trials, and above them, simultaneously; to both suffer and soar all at once; to be sorrowful, yet always rejoicing; to be weak and yet made strong (2 Cor. 6:10; 12:9–10).

As for me, most days seem made for walking. These are days of ordinary routine, days of repetitive tasks and persistent problems, days when we are asked to resist the next temptation, finish the next task, prepare the next meal, enjoy the next pleasure, read the next chapter, pray the next prayer, get the next cancer treatment. Just like in everyday life people walk more than they run or soar, even so, I think that God-strengthened walking is the normal Christian experience in our pilgrimage toward our heavenly Home.

Besides, I'm not finding it easy to run or soar these days. Multiplied burdens, diseases, and sorrows will do that to you. So I have to be content with walking. Not that I mind. For real life is mostly about putting the next foot in front of the last.

If you show me one of those ever-popular wall-hangings with a soaring eagle, captioned with "they shall mount up with wings like eagles" it will inspire. But I think I'd be much more moved by a painting of a walking saint, far along a roughly hewn path, winding through hill and valley, storm and stillness, desert and oasis, swamp and garden, forest and plain, all-the-while with his eye beholding Isaiah's God and fixed on The Heavenly City. Add the caption, "they shall walk and not faint" and I'd be awed. This is the amazing ever-sufficient daily grace of God.

What I know is that at some point in all of our lives we will need each of these: strength to run, to soar, and to walk. So let us hold onto the promise that God will measure out just the right amount of grace when the time comes.

Cliff-Hanger or Climax?

"For behold, I create new heavens
  and a new earth,
and the former things shall not be remembered
  or come into mind.
But be glad and rejoice forever
  in that which I create;
for behold, I create Jerusalem to be a joy,
  and her people to be a gladness.
I will rejoice in Jerusalem
  and be glad in my people;
no more shall be heard in it the sound of weeping
  and the cry of distress."

Isaiah 65:17–19

As I close my Isaiah 40 meditations, I realize that I am on a long, long, long, long pilgrimage. Similar to Israel who was exiled to Babylon for 70 years, and became desperate for Isaiah 40-like comfort, I, too, have been in a very long season of trial, and am desperate for comfort, as well.

My life is measured in big numbers now. I am 66 years old. I was converted to Christ 51 years ago, which began my arduous faith journey "through many spiritual dangers, toils, and snares." While full of joys, nearly every step of the way has also been on a tear-moistened path.

I need big numbers to measure my trials, too. I've had at least a 6.5 degree headache everyday and all day for over 12,775 straight days. I've lived with, and been treated for, stage 4 cancer everyday for 730 straight days. I've had significant back pain for at least 3,000 straight days. I've had a severe bone infection for nearly 365 straight days. I've been hooked up to my despised, quality-of-life-reducing intravenous medical pack for 320 straight days.

And perhaps most distressing of all is that I have no idea how or when any of these is going to end. My story is a cliff-hanger, and my journey through the shadowlands is incomplete. I am still waiting on the Lord and he is still renewing my strength. But who knows what is going to happen next?

I'm like Paul. I don't know whether I'm going to die and experience the gain of seeing Jesus, or live on to have more fruitful labor in the Lord (Phil. 1:20–24). I've got answers for nothing. I don't know how long I'll live. I don't have any idea whether my diseases will take me, or my God will heal me.

All I can do is draw daily consolation from the well of God's character and comfort, as revealed in Isaiah 40, and then take the next step with my eyes looking upward and my heart set on Home.

Which reminds me that in the ultimate sense, my story really isn't a cliff-hanger. I may not know when my life will end, or what means God is going to use to bring about that end. But I do know how it's all going to turn out in the life to come. It's all going to end with a brand new beginning!

Just like God promised ancient exiled Israel a longed-for return to Jerusalem, their earthly home, even so he has promised me—and all who believe—a better Jerusalem and Heavenly Home. Our Home is Mount Zion, the New Jerusalem, the coming Heavenly City of the Living God; where the God of Isaiah 40 lives in person to be our comfort and healing forever (Isa. 66:17–19; Heb. 11:13–16; 12:22–23; 13:14; Rev. 21:1–5, 22–23; 22:1–5).

And herein lies the greatest comfort of all. We have a Shepherd-Ruler who will gather us up as lambs in his arms, being mighty to carry us all the way Home; to an eternal Abiding Place where the "sound of weeping and cry of distress will be no more." On that day, every tear and trial will be a "former thing" never to be remembered again. In that place, everything will be made new, and we will be his joy, and he will be ours, forever and ever. Amen.

Until then, the God of Isaiah 40 will keep comforting us by revealing to us his glorious character and love, and by keeping his promise to renew our strength so we can run, soar, and walk, until we finish the course and arrive all the way Home (2 Tim. 4:7–8).

So this isn't a cliff-hanger after all. Instead it's a

foreshadowing of our story's wonderful climax, when before our wondering eyes, we shall behold God as he is, and we will never need to be comforted again.

Acknowledgments

I would like to thank those who have encouraged me to write this book. Thank you Bob Feldman for your early and frequent encouragements to publish parts of my journal. Thank you Janel Feldman for your masterful proofreading skills. Thank you Benjamin Vrbicek for inviting me on to the Gospel-Centered Discipleship team and encouraging my writing so enthusiastically—not to mention helping me put this simple work together. Thanks to all of you who previewed and endorsed this work. Thank you David Wangaard for your relentless encouragement to embrace my keyboard as my new pulpit.

And thank you dearest Gayline, for holding my hand time and again as we've paused and stood together to behold our God, lost in shared wonder, love, and praise.

About the Author

Tim Shorey has followed Jesus for over fifty years. He and his wife, Gayline, have enjoyed forty-seven years together, with six children and fourteen grandchildren. Soon after his fortieth year of pastoral ministry, Tim was diagnosed with stage 4 cancer, with an uncertain prognosis. Not long thereafter, he also contracted a rare, severe, and, as yet uncured, bone disease.

Now in medically-caused retirement, Tim spends his limited energy delighting in family and friends, writing, composing songs of sadness and joy, and preaching occasionally (from a chair) as God enables. He keeps an expanding Caring Bridge cancer journal, currently with over 1,000 entries and 150,000 visits, and he writes numerous articles for The Gospel Coalition and Gospel-Centered Discipleship. Besides *From a High Mountain*, Tim has authored *Respect the Image: Reflecting Human Worth in How We Listen and Talk*; *30/30 Hindsight: 30 Reflections on a 30-Year Headache*; *A Communion Truce: How Holy Communion Addresses Our Unholy Conflicts*; *An ABC Prayer to Jesus: Praise for Hearts Both Young and Old*; and *Worship Worthy: Alliterative Adoration*.

You may visit his From My Youth website at timothyshorey.com.

From My Youth Resources

From My Youth is the broader ministry platform for all of Timothy M. Shorey's writing, including . . .

Worship Worthy: Alliterative Adoration (Independently Published)

30/30 Hindsight: 30 Reflections on a 30-Year Headache (Independently Published)

An ABC Prayer to Jesus: Praise for Hearts Both Young and Old (Redemption Press)

Respect the Image: Reflecting Human Worth in How We

Listen and Talk (P&R Publishing)

A Communion Truce: How Holy Communion Addresses Our Unholy Conflicts (Gospel-Centered Discipleship)

From a High Mountain: 31 Reflections on the Character and Comfort of God (Based on Isaiah 40) (Independently Published)

Broken but Beautiful: Reflections on the Blessings of the Local Church, a contributing author (Gospel-Centered Discipleship,)

His Way with Words, assorted blogposts (From My Youth, timothyshorey.com, website)

Thou Art the Potter, a public daily journal leading readers into and through Tim's cancer experience at https://www.caringbridge.org/visit/timothyshorey.

Out of the Depths: Songs of Sadness and Joy, a collection of original songs and personal psalms composed by the author while in the furnace of his trials, tentatively scheduled for release, pending God's provision, in mid to late 2025.

A growing collection of sermons.

To my Mom, Elsie Akers,
who provided a loving home
for twelve children.
I also thank God
for bestowing His gift
of my creative mind.

Chapter 1

Seventeen year old Brittany had grown up in Breenville, a typical tiny mid-western town where everyone knew everyone else. Their single and two-story houses were mostly bordered with colorful flowers dripping over wooden fences neatly painted every two years. And their town had its requisite little square with a statue of a noted local man in the center of four blocks of tiny stores with benches, bushes and occasional spots of landscaping attempts in front of the fancier stores.

Being constantly together, people had begun to resemble one another as very average folk. All except for Brittany. Even though she was still only a high school senior, she stood out because of her extraordinary beauty. Her blue-black hair, black as night, and as shiny as a dark pool in the midnight, swished around her as she walked with a stride that belied her lack of confidence. Her eyes, the blue of a clear sky on a sunny day, revealed an innocence of life's shadier experiences. She was not aware that she drew the gaze of every man in Breenville -- especially the eyes of Blake Daniels.

Blake Daniels also stood out from the rest. Not only was he one of the most handsome twelfth graders, but he walked with the gait of one who considers himself a winner. His dark, wavy hair was never out of place. His long, tan body spoke of dedicated exercise. He knew he could have any girl of his choosing, but he focused only on Brittany. Everyone noticed he would do anything just to steal a moment with her. She ruled his heart and mind. Although they had always

1

been good friends, Blake now wanted so much more. He was vulnerable where she was concerned. His biggest fear was of losing her.

Brittany did not encourage him and repeatedly protested, "Let's just be friends, OK Blake?" She refused to acknowledge that she melted whenever she saw him.Because she guarded this secret not only from him, but from everyone else she knew, even her face never revealed how giddy she felt in his presence. Sometimes, when he looked at her, she would suddenly feel awkward and become clumsy, losing her footing or bumping into objects. Though she knew nothing of love, her mind daily wove romantic fantasies in which Blake would be the leading character.

Eveyone thought they were a pair, but because she was so adept at hiding her feelings, people failed to notice her lack of confidence. They did not see the vulnerability in her gaze. When she thought about their relationship, she was sure she would not be the girl that would finally capture Blake's love. Surely she could never compete with all of the females that followed him around. She was acting as a best friend only to hold onto him, believing she would lose him if she showed more than friendship. She would settle for any time he would allow for them to be together.

The big senior dance was coming up, and the entire class was frantically involved in decoration and presentation preparations ever since they had rented out the large hall at The Breenville Social Club. The excitement of the student body and of anyone connected to the dance had reached fever pitch

All the girls were frantically shopping for the most beautiful dress of all. Brittany had already chosen her clothing – a floor-length silver chiffon gown with a fitted bodice and a single single strap to hold it up. Enhanced with light
2

blue sequins to offset her blue eyes, the gown was cut low in the front, showing off the cleavage that separated her well-rounded breasts. The back was open, showing her delicate back and sensuous curves. Now she faced only one problem. Regardless of how pretty she might look in her dress, no one had asked her to the dance.

This had never happened to her before. During all her years in high school, she had never missed a dance and had always been asked to partner the most popular males. Not this time. Even guys she knew didn't have dates weren't asking her. Having no idea why this was happening to her, she began to brood.

One evening, while she and her friend Lissa were in the midst of a homework session, she had begun to brood. She was so deep into her brooding that she did not even hear the phone ringing until Lissa snapped her out of it by bringing the phone to her ear. "The phone has been ringing and you have not even heard it? Yet, it's right next to you." Rolling her eyes with a dejected look, Brittany took the phone from Lisa.

Her eyes lit up when she heard the voice. "Hi, Brittany, this is Blake. What are you up to?"

She didn't answer him right away. She would tease him to see if he didn't yet have a date for the dance. If he even hinted he had not, she would ask him to take her to the dance. After all, what are friends for.

When she didn't answer, he repeated,"Brittany?"

She finally seemed to wake up. "Blake, I'm sorry. Now what were you saying?" She realized she needed to put aside her own thoughts and listen to what Blake had to say.

After clearing his throat, Blake began to speak again.

3

"Ahem. Uh, I was just wondering how you were. If I'm interrupting anything, I can always call back later."

Brittany's voice changed as she tried to placate him.
"No, of course not, Blake. I...uh...was just preoccupied with
something silly. You know how little things can make your
mind go off in a million directions."

That's exactly what Blake thought he was having. Silly
thoughts. He had been to dances with her before, but this one
somehow would be different. He felt a strong urge to be in a
closer relationship with her.   No matter how crazy he thought
his scheme might seem, he still had to take a chance to
make it a reality. He knew the deadline to prepare for the
dance had already been reached and passed and also knew
she did not have a date.

She had no idea the amount of trouble he had gone
through to make sure whe would go to the dance only with
him. All their friends were keeping his secret and helping him.
No one would ask her to the dance until he worked up the
nerve to ask her out for a real date. It was true the friends had
reluctantly given their OK to his request and had kept silent,
but he had won. She had no other date for the dance, though
a number of ther boys had really wanted to ask her.   They all
knew he was crazy about her.

He wiped the sweat forming on his forehead. "Well, I
was thinking about asking you to the dance if you don't have
a date yet." Not wanting to sound insulting, he added, "But
I'm sure you already do." Of course he knew the truth. His
friend Jack's girlfriend was one of Brittany's friends and she
had been keeping him informed. He was always glad to hear
his friends were keeping to his plan.

*Someone probably told him I didn't have a date and
he's being good and stepping up to rescue me.* Brittany was
4

feeling sorry for both of them. She hoped he wasn't breaking a date with somebody else to do this for her. She would feel absolutely terrible if he had.

"Actually, Blake, I don't have a date yet." She was so embarrassed she could feel the heat rising in her face and giving her a flushed complexion. "So... uh...sure, I'd be glad to go with you." She waited a few moments before asking, "Uh, you don't have a date either?"

"I sure don't," he answered with a tremor in his voice. "And the dance sounds like fun! I'll pick you up Friday evening around seven thirty. See you then!"

Brittany heard the click of Blake's phone when he hung it up, yet she still held on to her own phone. Was it her imagination, or did Blake sound nervous? Now, why in the world would he be nervous about asking her to a dance? They had been to at least a dozen dances together over the years.

She felt she should be the nervous one, knowing she had hoped all along that Blake would be the one to accompany her. She was pleased he had saved her the awful awkwardness of having to ask him to take her. But maybe he had asked her only because he was her friend and felt sorry for her. She wished for more.

Blake was beside himself with joy! He could hardly wait for the dance. On that night his dream of holding Brittany very close in his arms would finally come true. This night the dances mattered. True, he'd only be holding her for a couple of the slow dances, but he wanted to hold her very close forever. He congratulated himself. "I am the luckiest man alive!"

Chapter 2

Brittany stood in front of her full length mirror, questioning her choice of outfit for the dance. She wanted to look absolutely gorgeous, but she felt something was missing. Her accessories for the evening included a single diamond necklace with a matching tennis bracelet. Her hairstyle did not reflect the usual attempt at sophistication most girls would have chosen for the big dance. Instead, her gleaming hair cascaded like a waterfall across her shoulders and down her back. She knew Blake loved her hair because he had complimented her on it more than a few times and had often reached out to touch it. Since she didn't care much for make up, she wore very little, applying only a small amount of mascara and just a smidgen of light pink lipstick.

As she looked at her reflection in the mirror, she admitted she looked very pretty. Still, the longer she looked, the more she felt something was missing. Maybe a little something around the waist. Aahh, like perhaps Blake's arms. She imagined herself on the dance floor with him as he held her close to his heart. She would feel his warm breath caressing her ear and neck. She would smile as he whispered secrets into her ear. Her fingers would be entangled in his dark, wavy hair. She would be the envy of every female at the dance.

Lissa interrupted her thoughts. She had entered the room and Brittany had not even noticed her or heard her call out, "Brittany." When Lissa repeated it more loudly the next time, Brittany turned to face her friend with vaguely focused eyes. "Brittany," Lissa repeated.

6

When Brittany finally turned her face toward her friend, it was bright red. "Lissa, I didn't hear you come in," she answered softly.

Lissa chuckled. "Obviously." When she saw Brittany sneak one more glance into the mirror, she walked up close to her and whispered, "Oh, trust me, you have nothing to worry about, Brittany. You look absolutely stunning."

Lissa truly meant those words. As a matter of fact, everyone she knew thought Brittany was the most beautiful girl around. Blake or any other guy should count themselves lucky to have Brittany by their side.

Remembering why she had entered her friend's room in the first place, Lissa said, "Anyway, Blake is here and looking mighty handsome himself in his black tux. The two of you are going to blow the socks off everyone tonight."

The blush on Brittany's face reddened even more. "I was just standing here second-guessing my appearance. This is the dress I bought for the dance, but I was thinking it looks like it is missing something."

Lissa walked over to Brittany and stood beside her so that both their reflections were visible in the mirror. "Look at yourself, girl," Lissa urged. "Don't be silly. This dress flatters your perfect figure. Actually, you flatter this dress! You've nothing to worry about. Now, you get downstairs to that hunk of a man that's waiting for you before he starts thinking you're about to stand him up. I'll see you at the dance."

Blake already knew Brittany was the most beautiful woman he had ever laid eyes on. Yet, he had never seen her look as sensual as she did this very moment. He also knew he had to make sure she would be only his....his very own.

They were both very quiet on the way to the dance . Their only topics of conversation centered on their friends and what they speculated everyone would do after graduation. The subject of what either of them were going to do never came up.

Brittany felt relieved when they finally arrived at the dance. For some reason she had felt uneasy, even nervous, in the car with Blake. Now she was shaky, and her palms were moist with perspiration. She had noticed Blake also seemed uneasy. When he had turned to stare at her each time she spoke, she could feel his eyes burning through her.

She did feel a frisson of pleasure, though, realizing she was having an effect on him, even it what she was experiencing was nerve wracking.

Soon all their friends congregated around them, complimenting them as they made their entrance, as if everyone had been anticipating their arrival. The girls were eager to see Brittany's new dress. As usual, they had not been disappointed.

The music had already begun to play. Some of the students were on the dance floor as the strobe lights,bright and flashing, made shadows dance just as fast and hard as they were dancing. Now was the time, Blake thought, to ask Brittany for a dance before he lost his courage. He had danced with her many times before this evening, but never with these intense feelings buzzing inside of him. He needed to feel her in his arms.

Brittany felt lightheaded. She never dreamed it could feel this wonderful in his arms. It was as if their bodies were pieces of a puzzle that fit snugly together. She could feel the heat of his breath and the erratic beating of his heart against her own chest.

8

As Blake held Brittany, her body felt strong against his, but at the same time soft as velvet. The smell of her skin filled his senses. Her hair in his fingers felt like the finest of all silks. This was surely a dream come true. He actually reached and pinched his hand to confirm that it wasn't. He had felt the sting of his own pinch, so this was no dream at all..this was real. Very real.

Chapter 3: Four Years Later

Brittany and Blake had been accepted into the same college a little over four years ago. Landfair College was certainly not one of the biggest colleges, but it was a well- respected institution. Both sets of their parents had attended it, so it seemed fitting for them to choose the same college for themselves. Now Blake was a radiologist and Brittany was a registered nurse in the same place, Briars Memorial Hospital.

Over-protective of Brittany, Blake had moved into an apartment not far from hers. Although college had matured Brittany, Blake still thought she was naive about many things, especially when it concerned their relationship. He thought they should have moved in together or married a long time ago, but Brittany hadn't wanted to. Before graduation she had protested. "Blake, if we're together all the time, we might not apply ourselves to our studies. We still will spend much time together, but I need to focus one hundred percent on my studies, and I don't think I can with you in the same apartment."

Blake had patiently accepted her rationale. Maybe a live-in relationship could interfere with classes and studying. But now that they were out of school, he expected a different closeness. Nevertheless, Brittany turned him down again. This time the excuse was different. "I want to become established first on my own. I need to focus on my profession first. We have plenty of time later." Unhappily, he had agreed to wait a while longer.

Brittany had many friends. Just as in high school, she attracted a variety of people but was still closest to her oldest friend Lissa Hewitt. Although each had chosen a different path of life, they had remained friends after high school and kept in contact on a regular basis. Brittany was still very conservative, whereas Lissa was very outgoing and sometimes considered by others to be a party girl on the wild side.

When he asked Brittany how come she was still such close friends with a girl so different from her, Brittany answered, "She just kind of does her own thing. And that's partying. But I love her like a sister." She hesitated a moment before saying very quickly, "By the way, she's coming to visit for a few days."

Brittany could now hear Lissa singing in the shower. She knew that within minutes she would be coming down the hall in a scanty bikini pajamas asking what their plans were for the day. Lissa had absolutely no qualms about prancing around half nude. To her it was just the natural thing to do when it was "just the girls." Although Brittany protested that anyone could come visiting, Lissa said she didn't care.

Sure enough, less than five minutes later, Brittany looked up to see Lissa standing at her bedroom door, fluffing her hair with a towel. No matter how often this happened, Brittany still wasn't sure how she should react to her friend's behavior. She didn't want to sound stuffy, but she still didn't feel comfortable. "Lissa, why do you insist on not putting on some clothes? Has it ever occurred to you that maybe I and other people don't want to especially see a half-naked person prancing around?"

With eyes lowered, Brittany pretended to be more interested in her book than she actually was just to keep from looking at her friend. It wasn't that Lissa was bad looking, it

11

was quite the opposite. Maybe a man would have like to see her unclothed, but Brittany didn't feel comfortable.

Lissa's shoulder-length brown hair with sparkling light blonde highlights complimented her tanned complexion. Her shapely long legs seemed to go on forever until they reached her perfectly round seat. Her flat stomach made her firm breast appear even larger. Pretty much a work of art, Brittany thought, but it didn't mean she was comfortable having a conversation with a person who was rubbing the towel in her hair so vigorously it was making her breasts bounce with her movement. The sight was unsettling. And she knew Lissa would walk around all day the same way unless she had to get dressed to go out. If Blake came to visit, he would definitely disapprove.

Lissa stopped drying her hair and gave Brittany a sour look. She rested an arm on either side of the doorway allowing full view of her entire body. "Really, Brittany," she said, "I can't believe this still bothers you. I would have thought by now that sexy boyfriend of yours would have brought you out of your shell. I'm sure the two of you have been doing some exploring and have probably seen each other naked." Wiggling her nose at Brittany, Lissa gave a racuous laugh. "Besides it's no big deal. It's a body, and you have one just like it, only I think yours is better. Oh, don't get me wrong. I know my body is good, but I happen to think yours looks a little stronger and your breasts a tad more perky. You could walk around like that when Blake is here, and he might like it. Anyway, if Blake comes, I'll put something on." She laughed louder as she took the towel and wrapped it around her body. She enjoyed teasing her over-conservative friend.

Brittany tossed the book she had been holding at Lissa. It missed her, not because Brittany was a bad aim but because she really hadn't meant to hit her. This playful move caused Lissa to hop on the bed with her friend and start a pil-
12

low fight – something they hadn't done since high school. A few minutes later they were flat on their backs, laughing hysterically.

Later in the day,the two girls sat poolside, sipping raspberry smoothies. Lissa twirled her straw, licked it, pursed her lips, flapped her eyelashes, and smiled slyly at Bittany. "So, tell me about your life, Brittany.   Blake's a good-looking guy, and I bet he's got some wild moves going on. Care to share?" Lissa wiggled further down in her chair to be more comfortable, waiting to hear at least one juicy story from her friend.

The question did not shock Brittany. When they were teenagers, they had often fantasized verbally as they confided how they felt about boys they knew.   They had also shared stories of their first experiences in necking. Although she didn't mean to, Lissa sometimes seemed somewhat over-curious about Brittany's sexual relationship with Blake. She thought everyone should be open about their sex lives,whereas Brittany focused less on what others were doing.   Secretly, she sometimes thought Lissa was just looking for tips on something to do that she hadn't tried yet.

When she didn't answer Lissa, her friend sat up, shielding her eyes from the sun with her hand as she looked intently at her. "We'll?" she questioned, sounding impatient.

Sex with Blake had not been a top priority for Brittany. Some day she planned to marry him and didn't want their intimacy to be dulled before their wedding night. She had stuck with her plan not to go all the way with him. Now, Lissa was making her feel guilty about her decision.

"We don't do crazy things, Lissa. " Brittany knew immediately she was going to regret those words. Nervously, she smoothed a strand of hair that had managed to escape her pony-tail holder. She could tell by the look on Lissa's face that

13

her sex life with Blake was about to be examined by Lissa, the self-proclaimed sex expert.

Lissa's mouth flew open, and her chin dropped so low it looked s if it might touch her chest. "What in the world is that supposed to mean? As hot a couple as you two are, you don't expect me to believe that, do you? It's me, Brit, you don't have to be apprehensive about anything you say to me. Lord knows I'm not one to judge." Lissa reached for her smoothie and sucked the straw noisily.

Sex was a very delicate subject for Brittany, and she really didn't want to discuss it at all. But she knew if she didn't talk now with Lissa, she would be insistant until she shared something, so she might as well get it out of the way.

First, Brittany sat up in her chair and raised the back forward three clicks, which made her sit straighter. This was not necessarily a comfortable position, but it readied her for the quick escape she was planning. She would say just a few words on this matter,   then promptly rise and jump into the pool. "We, or I, I should say, prefer not to wear out the intimate side of the relationship before we can even get started on our marriage. And furthermore, I am not ready for children, or the duties of motherhood that accompany them." There, she had said it!

Lissa found it hard to believe what she had just heard. She sat frozen for a moment as her closest friend dove into the pool. Then she, too, jumped in after her and swam to Brittany, who had turned to float on her back. When Brittany heard the splash and felt Lissa's movements near her, she raised her head, dreading the continuation of the same topic of conversation. Swimming to the ladder, she hoisted herself to sit on the side of the pool.

Lissa followed, sitting beside her and continuing the conversation as if there had not been an interruption. "Oh
14

boy, Brittany, you'd better wake up. Blake is a man, and a darn good-looking one at that. I can bet you he's more than ready. Maybe not for fatherhood, but I'll guarantee he doesn't feel the same as you about wearing out the intimacy thing. I've seen the way he looks at you. He practically devours you with his eyes."

"Maybe you're right, Lissa, but if he has a different opinion, he doesn't mention it any more. He knows how I feel, and I think he's come to accept that." Her tone was nonchalant, as she began to wrap her hands around her wet hair to squeeze out the excess water as if what they were talking about were of no consequence.

"You say he doesn't mention it anymore? If I were you, I would wonder about that. I guess I just haven't ever trusted a man that much. My mind would be questioning if he was having his fun elsewhere while he's waiting on you to give in to him. You may want to rethink your logic about this." Instantly, Lissa regretted her words, hoping she had not sounded too harsh.

As she rose, Lissa's shadow shaded Brittany from the sun, causing her to shiver from the sudden chill. Brittany felt goosebumps on her body.

That evening, Lissa received an emergency call from the hospital where she worked. The nurse covering her shift had been in a car accident, and Lissa had to take over as soon as possible. Brittany was sad to see her go, although her earlier conversation left her somewhat troubled. She wasn't angry. Her relationship with Lissa had always been close and never allowed for anger, but somewhere hidden in her subconscious she had begun to feel twinges of warnings about something, though she could not say what. She shook her head. Maybe she was worried about Lissa being right about the problems she might have in not giving in to Blake.

15

In the days following Lissa's visit, Brittany gave her relationship with Blake some extra consideration. She certainly
didn't want to lose him, yet she could not believe he would
"mess around" with someone else. Finally, she decided she
wouldn't entertain this kind of thinking. She would serenely
prepare herself for her date with Blake that evening.

When she gave a final glance in the mirror, she liked
what she saw. The high-heeled shoes with straps around her
ankles showed off the muscular calves she had gained from
jogging every day. Her light pink silk blouse was just tight
enough to make the imagination run wild. The black skirt she
chose to wear was not quite a mini, but short enough to tease
Blake. As usual she decided to leave her hair down.

Maybe they would and maybe they wouldn't have sex
now, but she was determined to make Blake see her as a
sexy woman. Tonight she needed him to want her.

Blake was looking forward to this evening with Brittany.
He wanted to brave the subject again that had always been
taboo. For years, his feelings had only intensified.

When she opened the door, Blake tried to hold back
the urge to grab her and kiss her passionately, opting instead
to compliment her. "Brittany, you always look so lovely. And
tonight is no exception," Lovely was not exactly the first word
the had thought of when he saw her. It was more like sexy,
added by very sexy. He felt his pulse quicken as she eased
herself into the seat of his red Corvette.

As she moved, he caught a glimpse of her panties and
inner thigh. To remain a gentleman, he forced himself to avert
his eyes to her face, only to be tortured by the sight of her
moistening her full lips with her tongue. With much control, he
smiled, closed the car door, and hurried to the driver's side.
Seated close to her, he inhaled the faint aroma of Tresor per-
16

fume that filled his senses, nearly driving him over the edge.

She knew he was panting for her on the inside and she loved it. If only Lissa could see him now. She would take back those words about his being with someone else. She reached over and rested her hand on his. "Thank you, darling," she said, giving him a sultry grin.

Since the drive to the Chinese restaurant was a short distance, they had not had much time for small talk. Now seated at the table, Blake broke the silence. " I thought we could go down to the lake after dinner.The moon is full, and since it's such a clear night, the stars will be so bright. We could just sit and soak in the beauty. Feel like going with me?"

Brittany couldn't resist the intense look he was giving her. When he formed a teasing pout and sad eyes, she smiled. It was hard to say no, so she agreed to go, deciding she might have to fight him off only if she wanted to.

They talked about Lissa's visit and how it was too bad her trip had been cut short. Then they laughed about the nurse who had been found kissing a man in the waiting area of Briars Memorial Hospital where they both worked. The nurse later revealed the man was her husband who had just returned from an assignment out of town.

"The gossip and drama at the hospital is terrible, isn't it?" Brittany asked Blake.

Too involved with reading his fortune cookie to comment on the drama of the nurse, Blake merely smiled and nodded his head.   Handing her an unwrapped fortune cookie, he looked up at her. "Brittany, what wise words does your fortune cookie hold?"

Brittany unwrapped the cookie and chuckled. "Blake,

these things are just silly fun. They're not true. Anyway, mine says, 'The one who laughs the most, loves the most.' Now what is that supposed to mean? And yours?" She took a bite of her cookie.

Taking a sip of his wine to wash his cookie down, Blake replied, "We'll I guess it could mean that if you are in love, you laugh a lot." Reaching across the table, he touched her hair with his fingertips. "I guess then I should be hysterical as much as I love you, Brittany."

Brittany extended her body forward until her lips met his soft, gentle kiss. Blake felt the need inside him stir. He wondered how much more he could take of this tonight. When the kiss ended and he opened his eyes, he couldn't help but notice that her leaning forward was allowing the already low-cut blouse to fall even lower, revealing more of her perfect breasts.

When Brittany realized this, she quickly sat back against the chair. She felt a lady should not appear otherwise to any patron or waitress who just happened by. But she must admit that kiss had felt so good and her body was still tingling from it. She wanted to kiss him again but would wait for the privacy of Blake's car.

Raking his hand through his hair, and straightening his already neat shirt, Blake looked at her intensely and quietly whispered, "That was some kiss."

Pleased with herself so far, Brittany felt she had added a little spice to their relationship. She had only wanted to make sure Blake was interested solely in her and that his interest did not wane. Her innocent little game, as that was all it was to her, seemed to be working very well.

That evening the moon's reflection on the lake made

the area seem magical. Two moons existed in a perfect atmosphere of gentle breezes wafting the perfume of wildflowers and sweet grasses. The soft sussurring of forest animals and chirping birds relaxed the listeners as if they were listening to soft music. They could occasionally hear the faint barks of dogs from a distant hunting camp. Brittany sighed as she leaned against Blake. "It's truly beautiful here."

Blake's love for Brittany reflected in his eyes. Gently moving a stray hair from her face, he said, "Not anywhere as beautiful as you. Not one of those stars up there in that big sky outshines your beauty. I love you, sweet Brittany."

Curling herself up closer to Blake, Brittany placed her head on his shoulder. She felt warm and safe here. She looked up at him and stroked his chin. "I love you, too, Blake."

They spent the next few moments cheek to cheek, silently gazing at the stars. When Blake did speak again, there was a serious but still gentle tone to his voice. "There's something I'd like to discuss with you, Brittany." He maneuvered his body in a position so that Brittany was forced to lean more into his arms than on his shoulder.

When she looked up at him, she spotted a deliberate look in his eyes and felt her spirits sink as she instantly began to have doubts again about what Lissa had said. Was he about to confess something awful to her? She didn't say a word, only nodded, hoping his words would not leave her numb forever.

He brushed her cheek softly with the back of his hand, and she watched the mouth she had kissed a thousand times pronounce the next words. "We've been dating since we were, what, like seventeen, eighteen years old," he said looking out over the water. "You and I have managed to stay together longer than any of the people we've ever known. School. Col-

19

lege, moving, it's all been stressful. Even to the point of over-whelming at times." Not wanting to see her expression, he continued to watch the water lap the shoreline. "What about us, Brittany? Where are we going? Where are we right now? I feel like we are just stuck in this place, wherever this is. I want more from you, more of your time, more of you."

She felt him inhale a deep breath. She knew exactly what he was asking. He wanted them to live together, sleep in the same bed at night and have breakfast together in the morning. She just wasn't ready to commit to those things. "Blake," she began as she repositioned herself so that she was sitting straighter and facing forward. "I want that too. Believe me I do. We can do more things together, but the one thing you want from me is hard for me to do. Not because I don't love you or want you. I do. I just don't want to make a mistake, and mistakes do happen. We're still young. We have our whole lives ahead of us."

She saw he had turned his face away. He was avoiding her words, but she continued nonetheless. "I think things are fine the way they are. I mean, maybe we aren't intimate enough and I certainly don't want to lose you over that. I also don't want to be pressured. The consequences are very high when you consider I'm not ready to become a mother. That alone would be so unfair to a child." She put her face in her hands, not to cry, but to hide the fear she felt in her heart that she was sure he would see in her eyes.

Blake felt a pang of guilt in the pit of his stomach. He really hadn't thought her view of their relationship in that way. Of course she would be more concerned about the possibility of pregnancy. It would be her body going through a dramatic change and she would be the main person in the baby's life. Not that he wouldn't be there,because he would be, every step of the way. He would not want this happening to her unless she absolutely wanted it. He would have to be more un-
20

derstanding. God help him. It would be so much easier if she weren't so incredibly desirable.

Looking at her now, he felt the heat inside him rise. Reaching for her, he pulled her even closer. "I'm sorry, Brittany. I never want you to feel as if I'm pressuring you. I do love the time we spend together and the intimacy that we do share is out of this world." His hand rested at the rise of her breast. "You're beautiful," he continued, "and very hard to resist. I hope you understand where I'm coming from too. I love you, so much." He heard her moan as he kissed her passionately.

Chapter 4

Looking back on that evening a few months later, Brittany was more comfortable now in her relationship with Blake. She was glad they had had their much needed talk, and she no longer felt pressured. Strangely, she had begun to feel more passionate after their discussion. Little by little their relationship was growing into a more sensual bond.

They had planned a beautiful weekend to spend alone, away from others in the peaceful mountains, where they would be surrounded by nothing but the sounds of a lazy river and the sweet songs of the birds. They would build fires, take long walks, and go canoeing. She had been even more excited when the rental agency had told them they might get to see some wild animals wandering into the yard. "It's going to be a wonderful weekend, Blake," she had whispered after their plans had been finalized.

When Blake arrived at her house early Friday afternoon, she was ready with her overnight bags already packed and placed by the door. Feeling happier than he could ever imagine, Blake knocked, calling out "Brittany, I'm here, It's time to pull out of here. The cozy cabin in the woods is waiting!"

Brittany appeared from around the corner of her bedroom wearing jeans and a tank top. Her hair was held back in a pony tail. "I'm ready," she exclaimed! "Let's get this show on the road!"

Blake smiled at her enthusiasm and a little at the casual way she was dressed, which was unusual for her. She reminded him of a little girl going on her first camping trip. But Lord, looking at her, she sure didn't look anything like a little girl. He was one lucky man, he nearly said aloud.

The drive to the cabin revealed the magnificent beauty which seemed a prelude to a good time. The sun setting in the sky had given the few clouds a yellow orange glow. The trees looked majestic, while their leaves waving gently in the light breeze seemed welcoming. As they approached the cabin on the dirt road, they could see the river through the trees. Brittany decided this was the most beautiful place she had ever seen.

"Oh Blake, it's perfect." She latched on to his arm and gave it a squeeze. "What a beautiful postcard this place would make. I'm going to be taking a lot of pictures while we're here."

Perfection was precisely what Blake had been aiming for this weekend. Very excited about this time he would spend alone with her, he wanted it to be a time she would never forget.

"Let's go see the inside," Brittany squealed! Eagerly, she headed for the front door. "I bet it's just as awesome on the inside as it is on the outside."

With their arms loaded down with luggage, they entered the cabin. Brittany instantly dropped the bags she had carried .Turning around full circle, with her eyes raking everything at once, she exclaimed in amazement. "Look at this place! It seems so rustic, yet is so extravagant."

The floors, as well as the trim around every window and doorway were made of solid oak. The chandeliers had

23

been crafted to resemble wooden wagon wheels hung from the cabin's oak beams. A very spacious kitchen to the right of the entryway sported a long oak table with six high-back chairs.

Brittany stood in the middle of the master bedroom. "The place is fabulous. Thank you so much, Blake, for suggesting we come up here for the weekend. I'm so glad that for once we didn't allow our jobs to get in the way of something we had planned." She enthusiastically threw her arms around Blake's neck. "We still have some daylight left. Can we just take a short walk around the outside? Would you mind, Blake?" she asked, batting her eyelashes in a playful manner.

Blake enjoyed seeing the free-spirited side of Brittany. As they walked, he inhaled the brisk, fresh mountain air. He vowed to make her enjoy every minute of this weekend and all this place had to offer. Secretly he was also hoping to enjoy more of Brittany in that alluring master bedroom.

"It is gorgeous out there, isn't it, Blake?" Brittany was ready to step into a hot shower before they decided what to do for dinner. When Blake didn't answer, she entered the shower, turned on the water and allowed it to run over her hair and down her body. Seconds later, she heard the glass shower door click, which meant Blake had entered the shower with her."

She then heard his low voice near her. "Is this okay?"

No words could escape her mouth. She granted him permission to stay with only a nod of her head. With her back to him, she felt his hands grasp her hips and work their way up her sides. He reached around and cupped her breast in his hands. She moaned as his hot lips began to kiss her neck. She backed into him so their bodies touched. She felt the hardness of him against her and gasped. The length of him
24

amazed her.

Blake then spun her around to face him. He wanted to see her face full of need for him. His mouth made contact with hers as he kissed her hungrily. It had been well over three months since he had been so close to her. When he lowered his mouth to her breast, she threw her head back. He knew she was wanting more.

Brittany knew she should stop him. Yet she allowed him to explore more of her body as he planted quick, soft kisses. He heard her moaning and release of a low scream. and knew she was so close to fulfillment. He knew he was driving her mad.

Although she was experiencing great pleasure, she also felt a battle of logic raging inside her. Her mind was demanding her to have Blake stop, but her body screamed for him to keep going. She tried to force herself to reason, but could only visualize making love with Blake. This one time she would succumb to this wonderful pleasure Blake was so freely giving her. Before she had time to think another thought, her world began to spin. Explosive sensations ran through her body as she filled both her hands with Blake's hair.

Blake carried her to the bed and gently patted her dry with a towel. "I love you," he said as he pressed his lips to hers.

"I love you too," she replied seductively while wrapping her legs around his. Yes, this one night she would not let her logical side win. She would not let it interfere with the unimaginable pleasure she was receiving from Blake.

They made love, losing all track of time. When their worlds exploded and crashed together, Brittany silently cried. She wasn't quite sure why, but guessed it must be from all the love she felt at that moment.

He spotted the woman in the woods examining the leaf she held in her hand and rolled it between her fingers. By the look on her face, she was apparently surprised by its feel. His heart skipped a beat as he took notice of her beauty. He had never seen such an exquisite face. Instantly his lighthearted mood changed as he noticed the man hurrying to catch up with her.

She was taken. That was just his bad luck! Some day he hoped to find a woman with such rare beauty. Some day he would. Yes, one day, he, Adam Franklin would.

Chapter 5

Since that romantic weekend, Blake and Brittany had spent many more nights together. Little by little, Brittany was learning to let go of her inhibitions, and Blake felt their relationship was better than ever. She had even begun to work on their wedding plans.

They finally decided on a fairly large wedding with family and friends they had kept in touch with from their home town. It would be somewhat on the extravagant side, but the expense was of no concern to either of them. Both were excelling in their jobs at the hospital.

Blake was definitely in higher spirits these days, feeling more joy than ever, and giving Brfittany all the credit for his happiness. Considering himself a lucky man, the thought of marrying Brittany was foremost in his mind. He would go to the end of the world for her. No one would ever take her from him. He had waited so long for her to realize they should always be together. His anxiety about their relationship had begun to nurture a jealousy he had never experienced before. He found himself disapproving of every man who stared at her. At times, he had even begun to show his disapproval.

In the last few weeks, the personnal at the hospital had experienced much stress from the incredible number of emergencies. The staff sometimes found it a hardship to keep up with the type of illnesses coming in. A large number of patients had been admitted because of an outbreak of a foreign strain of flu. In addition, the hospital staff had seen some of the worst injuries during the past week.   It was sometimes hard for the personnel to remain detached and not become emotionally involved with the people who needed care.

Brittany loved her job and enjoyed taking care of people. Yet, today she felt stressed. She couldn't decide if it was because of how busy she was or how strange Blake had been acting these last few days. All she knew was that something was taking a toll on her nerves.

She didn't understand why, when things were going so well between them, Blake had suddenly become very clinging. Even though he spent only a couple of nights a week with her, she was beginning to feel smothered. When he didn't stay, she had always assumed he went home. That was, until one night when she was having trouble sleeping and she noticed his car in the parking lot of her apartment complex. She had gone outside thinking something must be wrong, but she was shocked by Blake's answer when he told her he just thought she would be safer if he was nearby.

Nearby? He only lived a couple of blocks away! She had insisted he go home and convinced him that if she needed him, she would certainly call.

Today was the absolute worse. A small boy was brought in by an ambulance followed by the local police. A neighbor had called the police saying she believed the boy was being harmed. She could not have been more right. He appeared to have been beaten pretty badly.

He was terribly bruised. At this time, his parents were in custody and denying any accusations of abuse.   Looking at the boy's X-rays, Blake noticed that the child had a broken arm as well as two broken fingers. Children's Services was looking into placing him with foster parents, but for now, he was being admitted to the hospital.
28

After work, Brittany stopped by to see the little boy in his room. She wanted him to know he was safe here and that if he needed anything, he could ask for her personally. He told her his name was Scotty, and then began telling her about things he liked to do. His favorite pastimes were reading and and watching cartoons. She ended up spending most of her evening with him.

She noticed that as he reacted with her, he never once smiled. Even more strange was that he did not ask for or even mention his parents. By the time she was ready to leave, she had managed to get a few smiles from him, but his freckled, elfin face touched her heart. Before she left, she promised to visit him again soon.

For the next few days, Brittany visited Scotty several times a day. On the day he was discharged, she was surprised to see he had foster parents, Mr. and Mrs. Brooks, who seemed like a lovely couple. They agreed to allow her continued visits.

She found out later that Child Services had been looking for a family member to look after Scotty and care for him. He had an uncle, Adam Franklin, who had moved out of state a few months ago, and they were trying to locate him now. Brittany wondered if the uncle would show this little boy the love he so needed.

Scotty held tightly to Brittany's hand. "When will I see you again?" he asked her. "You're a lot of fun." When he looked up at her, she could have sworn she saw tears forming in his eyes.

Brittany knelt down so her face was even with his. "I'll be seeing you real soon. Don't you worry about that, sweetheart. Mr. and Mrs. Brooks are very nice people. They will take such good care of you."

Brittany felt him trembling as he threw his arms around her neck and hugged her tightly. Peeking over her shoulder at the two strangers who were taking him away from her, Scotty prayed they would be as nice as Brittany.

Knowing how much Scotty had come to mean to Brittany, Blake tried to be supportive of this situation. He was sure Scotty needed all the love he could get, but he was taking too much of Brittany's time. She was spending every free moment she had with the boy and he was beginning to resent that.

Chapter 6

Brittany wished Blake would be more considerate of how she felt about Scotty. "Blake, I told you that the child had great need of friendship right now. He's a very frightened little boy that has had his entire world turned upside down. He's confused, he misses his parents and on top of that he thinks this is all somehow his fault. Please, be patient. He's lonely and he's only seven years old."

"How can he be so lonely?" Blake argued. "When you're not with him, the Brooks are. Let them give him the attention he needs. You're getting yourself too involved. I don't want to see you get hurt. What happens when this uncle of his shows up and takes him away? Then what?"

Blake's attitude had become an annoyance. Brittany did not want him trying to dictate what she should do about Scotty. Deciding she was more than capable of making her own decisions, she answered him in anger. "Maybe you should consider spending some time with him! It might help you to be more compassionate towards this poor child. When the uncle shows up, I'll back off IF I feel Scotty is ready for me to do just that!"

"Fine," shouted Blake! "You do whatever you think you need to do, but just know that I am not at all thrilled about this!" Grabbing hold of the door, he swung it open, ready to storm out. Brittany's next words stopped him in his tracks.

In a somewhat calmer voice, Brittany spoke. "Today is

the first day of court for Scotty's case. I'd like you to be there. I know you don't have to testify about his X-rays yet, but Scotty will be held in the Judge's chambers during this time and I thought maybe you'd like to join me while I wait with him. He won't feel so alone." Brittany sat down and sank into the soft leather recliner, suddenly feeling exhausted from fighting with Blake.

Seeing Brittany looking so tired softened Blake's mood, but he still held his ground. "I might be there," he said. "I just do not want to get too involved with this little boy."

As he stomped out the door, he heard Brittany say that she hoped to see him there.

Brittany and the Brooks kept Scotty occupied while court was in session. Brittany did manage to be in the court-room when Mrs. Fields, Scotty's mother, took the stand. After hearing the woman speak, Brittany concluded that the woman's logic was pure craziness. In one outburst, Mrs. Fields expressed how much she wanted her son to come home. That statement was belied when, in the next breath, she said how stressful it was to raise a child and was glad to have been given a break. She also admitted that sometimes she did take a drink to calm her nerves. With a sly smile, she looked at the judge and said, "It's probably good for the child when I take a drink. I am calmer." Unfortunately, the court learned as she began to elaborate that Scotty's parents were alcoholics who abused their child.

When questioned, the Fields admitted that on the day Scotty had been beaten they "might have had a little too much to drink." They protested that the drinking was not the reason all of the problems had happened.

On the stand, Mrs. Fields declared, "Scotty just got in the way. Mr. Fields became angry when he thought I had
32

drunk two more beers than he had. Uhm. We had run out of beers." She smiled and lifted up her eyes innocently. "I guess our tempers had been very high. And, uh...we began to argue. Scotty came into the room and tried to make us stop. I guess he wanted to show us the new toy his Uncle Adam had just sent him."

The judge interrupted and asked, "And how did Scotty get hurt?" As the jury listened, the whole unsavory story unfolded.

Mrs. Fields lowered her eyes and then again opened them wide. "Well, Mr. Fields took the toy and threw it. It broke, and Scotty began to cry. I yelled at Mr. fields for treating him that way." She held her head sideways and fluttered her eyelashes. "Well, he became even more angry. I guess I shouldn't have interrupted, because he began to hit Scotty, saying he had been rude for interrupting him. Mr. Fields looked at me when he said that. He hates to be interrupted, you see."

"What happened then, Mrs. Fields?"

"Well, I yelled at Mr. Fields, and then he began to hit me. His anger went to a higher level. Now we both had interrupted him. And he doesn't like to be interrupted."

The judge twisted his lips, leaned forward and lifted up his eyebrows. "And how did you react, Mrs. Fields?"

"Well, then I became angry, too."

The judge sat back until he heard her next words. "I became angry beyond control and then I reacted, too. I began to scream and curse at Scotty and slap him on the head and face and then punch him in the stomach. But I was not the one who kicked him, judge. When he fell to the floor, his daddy kicked him because his crying had disturbed his day."

"And what happened next?"

"Why then, Mr. Fields walked out of the room."

The jury recalled hearing that when the neighbors had become concerned and called the police after hearing the altercations and the terrorized crying of the child, Scotty had already been hurt very badly.

Brittany silently prayed that the courts would see the Fields' home would never again be a place for Scotty. Where in the world was this uncle Adam Franklin that everyone spoke of so highly?

Adam Franklin had come in late and was sitting in the back. When he came in, he could not believe his eyes. There she was, sitting in the courtroom. She looked even more beautiful than he remembered. But what did she have to do with his nephew? No matter how hard he had tried to erase her from his memory, he had failed. And right now he was wondering if she was still with the man he had seen her with at the cabin.

Adam had been devastated to hear the words of the neighbors who had called the police on that awful day. When he spoke to the Brooks, they told him Scotty was in bad shape, but he had not imagined the extent of the boy's suffering. It was worse than he had imagined. He knew his sister and brother-in-law had a drinking problem, but never in his wildest dream would he have thought they would harm Scotty. How long had his precious nephew suffered at their hands? He was here now, willing to give his nephew the home he deserved, filled with love. Adam stood up and made his way to the Judge's chambers.

Brittany knew she needed to get back to the hospital.

With a heavy heart, she left the courtroom, intending to catch up with Scotty later. Once outside, she decided to take a moment to gather herself. Drawing in the fragrance of honeysuckle blooming nearby, she raised her face to the sky and allowed the sun to warm her. She had felt so cold sitting in that courtroom, listening to the frightful things two people with obviously disturbed minds had done to their own child. She knew she would never be able to understand any of it.

Scotty's face was radiant when he saw his Uncle Adam enter the Judge's chambers. Running so hard to embrace him, he threw Adam off balance. Scotty shrieked with laughter while Adam over-exaggerated the mishap for the fun of it.

"Uncle Adam," exclaimed Scotty when he finally stopped laughing! "Did you come to take me home with you? I don't think I'm allowed to live with Mommy and Daddy any more."

Adam saw the sadness in this child's eyes. What had they done to this wonderful little boy he loved so dearly? Before Adam could ask, Scotty bowed his head as a tear rolled down from his eyes. "They hurt me, Uncle Adam. I don't think they meant to, but could I stay with you?"

Adam felt his heart shatter into a million pieces. Wanting to reassure the boy by expressing his love for him, he lifted up his nephew until they were eye to eye. With a gentle voice that tried to hide his deep emotions, he said "I love you, Scotty. I'm here for you, and everything will be okay now. We're going to have a nice house with lots of love, and no one will ever hurt you, ever again."

Now the dam of tears Scotty had been trying to hold back rolled down the boy's cheeks. "They even broke my toy you sent to me. Now I don't have it any more." He hid his head by burrowing it into his uncle's shoulder.

Adam lifted up Scotty's face and wiped the tears with his handkerchief. Then he sat down, held him in his lap and smiled at him. "I'll just have to get you another one, won't I? Would that be okay?"   He would do everything in his power to show this child all the good that grownups could do for children. The anger for his sister and her husband boiled in his veins for how they had hurt Scotty.

Scotty felt much better now that his uncle was here, but he still wanted to see Brittany, too. "Uncle Adam," he said, "you have to meet my new friend. You'll like her a lot. She's very nice. And pretty too! She came to visit me in the hospital and read books to me."

"Well," answered Adam, "you'll just have to introduce me to this new friend of yours. I'll have to thank her for being so kind to you." Adam held him close for a moment and roughed up the boy's hair with his hand.

"Can you stay right here for just a moment?" Adam asked him. "I need to discuss something with the Judge and the Brooks. It will only take a minute. Okay, little man?"

Scotty watched anxiously as his uncle spoke to the other grownups. He hoped he was going with Adam instead of the Brooks.

When the judge asked Adam if he had somewhere to go with Scotty,   Adam explained that he still owned a home here. He also told the judge and the Brooks that he would have no problem transferring his practice as emergency room physician to Briars Memorial Hospital.   He had lived here before and had established a good reputation. Adam said he could also provide good home help for himself and Scotty and establish a stable and happy home life for the boy.

After considering all the facts, the judge decided it would be best for Adam to have Scotty. He was family, the boy wanted to be with him, the doctor seemed to have an excellent reputation and resources, and he wanted the boy.

Hand in hand, Adam and Scotty happily left the courtroom together. That was when Adam spotted her again. His mind returned to the very first time he had seen her. Somehow he was going to have an introduction to this woman.

Scotty would have spotted Brittany, but he had been too interested in the baby ducks walking across the courthouse lawn. He was calling to his uncle to see them. Adam was so enthralled with Brittany, he did not hear his nephew until Scotty tugged on the bottom of his
jacket. "Uncle Adam,' he spoke excitedly, "did you see the baby ducks?"

Adam forced his eyes away from her to answer his nephew. "No, Scotty, I'm sorry, I didn't. I was thinking about something else." He mussed Scotty's hair, asking "Where would you like to eat this evening?"

As Scotty thought of his answer, Adam again looked in the direction where Brittany had been standing, but she was gone.

Scotty finally chose three slices of cheese and pepperoni pizza, After that, he still managed to devour a large dish of chocolate ice cream. All the while, he chattered about his friend Brittany and about all the times she had brought him here and the fun time they had together.

Chapter 7

The next morning Adam took Scotty to the Brooks, promising to return after his visit with the chief of staff at Briars Memorial Hospital. The meeting could not have gone any better. Dr. Wayne, Chief of Staff, had welcomed him back and asked him to start as soon as possible. Now standing in his old office, it seemed as if he had never left. With no tasks pending at the moment, Adam decided to take a walk around the hospital and say hello to friends he hadn't seen in a while.

When he wallked into the cafeteria, he caught sight of the man he recognized with the beautiful girl from the cabin. Curbing his curiosity to ask about the girl, he introduced himself and made small talk for a while. After speaking with him for a few moments, he said, "It's been nice talking with you Blake. Maybe we could have a drink after work some time. That is, unless you have a wife waiting for you at home." This was his way of finding out if the woman was married to Blake Daniels.

Very nonchalantly, Blake smied and answered, "No, no wife yet. So a drink after hours would be just fine. I'll be seeing you around. Nice to have met you."

Adam was elated. Blake had not married the woman, nor had he mentioned even dating her. Hopefully they were a thing of the past. He had wanted to ask more questions, but he didn't want Blake to be curious as to why he was so interested in his old girlfriend.

Brittany had also seen him entering the hospital this

morning and now exiting the cafeteria. Since dating Blake, she rarely paid attention to other men. However, she had not failed to notice this unusually handsome man with jet black hair, brawny build and self-confident walk. He seemed in control of his life.

She must be overtired or really missing Blake, she speculated. Otherwise she would not be standing here in the middle of her workplace ogling a stranger. Or it could be that she was still upset at Blake for showing up at the courthouse only to tell her she should let the system deal with Scotty? He made it a point to dictate to her again not to be so involved in the boy's life. She really did not understand what had gotten into him to become so possessive lately.

The sounds of sirens interrupted her thoughts as she headed toward the ER. Patients were being brought in from a car accident that involved eight people. As nurses and doctors flitted from patient to patient, The ER became as hectic as a beehive. She cried out for someone to page at least one more doctor to the ER.

As she tried to comfort an expectant mother who had hit her head on the passenger side window, a doctor walked in. The woman didn't appear to be injured, just very shaken. As the physician walked over, his eyes never left the expectant mother's chart, and without looking up asked how she was doing. When Brittany turned to answer him, she saw the stranger she had noted before. *It's him. He's a doctor and he's standing right here in front of me. I can almost reach out and touch that soft black hair. What a sensuous mouth he has. What am I thinking?*

His agitated voice snapped her back into reality. "Nurse," he scolded! "What's the problem? I asked you a question." Adam raised his eyes form the chart, only to find himself staring into the most beautiful set of eyes he had ever seen. He felt he should apologize for being so abrupt, but he couldn't speak.

Brittany was the one to break the silence. "She's doing fine," she answered, her heart beating rapidly. "All of her vitals are normal. She appears to me more nervous than anything."

Adam was too stunned to speak. He did manage to finish with his patient before he turned again to Brittany, "Keep up the good work, nurse. Maybe dinner sometime?" he added before thinking. He quickly left the room.

The patient and Brittany looked at one another in utter confusion. In the hallway, safely away from her, Adam felt he had made a fool of himself. What made him act so unprofessionally? He never had before. He couldn't even remember if he had spoken to the patient. All he could think of now was that this beautiful woman must think him a complete imbecile.

Brittany was embarrassed and tried to apologize for the doctor's actions. But the expectant mother wouldn't hear of it. She chuckled instead. "I think that doctor was quite taken with you." When she saw Brittany's incredulous expression, she added, " Well, he WAS falling all over himself. After he looked at you, he forgot all about me. But I'm not offended. I think it's wonderful when a woman's beauty can cast a spell on a man." She patted her swollen belly. "How do you think I got this? Swept my husband right off his feet, I did. He had the same reaction when he first met me as your doctor there. It's great. I wonder if he realizes yet that he asked you out to dinner?"

Brittany fluffed the pillow and put it behind the mother's head. "He DID ask me to dinner, didn't he? I thought I imagined that." Brittany gave a little wry smile.

"He certainly did," the mother answered as she leaned

40

back into the pillow to feel more comfortable. She gave Brittany a wink. "And you should accept. Did you see how that gorgeous hunk of man looked at you? Don't pass that up, girl." She took a deep breath and closed her eyes. "Aaaahhh, new love."

When Brittany's shift ended, she went in search of the new doctor. Although she looked in a number of places he might be, she couldn't locate him but found Blake instead. When he asked her out for an early dinner, she hesitated. Still chafing from his earlier attitude toward her involvement with Scotty, she wasn't in the mood to be in his company. The dinner was not successful. Although they made an attempt at small talk during dinner, twenty minutes of almost total silence passed before she feigned a headache and excused herself for the evening.

Brittany drove to the Brooks' home, only to hear Scotty was not with them but would now be with his uncle. She was relieved to hear the uncle had made it. Realizing that Scotty needed time with his uncle, she drove home.

When she arrived home, she discovered a message on her answering machine from Scotty. inviting her to "the ice-cream place" to meet his uncle. After checking the time the call had come in, she glanced at her watch and decided that she could still meet them at seven. It was only six-thirty., and she could make it if she hurried.

Pulling into the parking lot, she immediately spotted Scotty. His smile was so bright as called in his trilling little voice, "Uncle Adam, she's here!"

Adam was paying the cashier and had not turned around yet when Scotty leaped into Brittany's arms. Scotty's action was unexpected, and Brittany squealed with joy, although she had to grab hold of the nearby table. Adam

41

whipped around to see what all the noise was about. When their eyes met again, neither spoke a word, but they both had smiles on their faces.

"Uncle Adam!" Scotty exclaimed, "This is my special friend, Brittany." He then pointed to Adam and said to Brittany, "And this is my Uncle Adam."

Without a word, and never taking his eyes off her, Adam began to walk towards her. "Guys," Scotty said. "Will somebody say something? Like hello!"

"Oh, well, Scotty," murmured Adam, "we briefly met at the hospital today." Remembering his gaffe when he had met her earlier that day, Adam felt a little uncomfortable.

"You mean you guys already know each other?" Scotty asked innocently.

Brittany was the first to answer. "I had no idea he was your uncle, Scotty. Anyway, we had not been properly introduced."

"This is quite a surprise. For the both of us, I'm sure," Adam said as he made the gesture for Brittany to sit down. "Please, may I get you a soda or something?"

"A soda, please," Brittany answered as she took a seat next to Scotty, who was staring at them strangely.

They sat and talked and laughed with Scotty for nearly a hour. Neither Brittany nor Adam asked each other personal questions, but kept their conversation centered around Scotty.

Even as young as Scotty was, he got the feeling they liked each other – in a boyfriend-girlfriend kind of way. They kept looking at each other in a funny way. Well, he hoped they
42

did. It would be nice for Brittany to be his uncle's girlfriend. Then he could spend time with both of them. None of them realized all three were thinking the same thoughts at the same moment, although Brittany was struggling against the idea.

Chapter 8

What had she been thinking? She could not believe she had just accepted a dinner date with Adam! He had completely caught her off guard. One minute they were discussing Scotty and the next minute he was asking her to dinner. She tried to tell herself she had accepted only because she didn't want to disappoint Scotty. That was of no use. If she was honest with herself, she would say it was because she wanted to know more about Adam. Blake was going to be furious.

It had been another long day at Briars Memorial, and Brittany was exhausted. The only thing that kept her going was thinking of the dinner she would be sharing with Adam. The entire day, a battle had been raging inside her. She kept telling herself it was just a dinner. Nothing more. It wasn't as if she was doing anything wrong." Dinner, just dinner," she told herself over and over again.

Earlier in the day she had seen Blake and told him she was going to meet with Scotty's uncle in the evening. She hadn't been exactly honest, because she neglected to mentioned Scotty wouldn't be joining them. Why hadn't she just told Blake the truth? For a moment she thought she must have asked that aloud. She had been in such deep thought that she jumped to hear Blake's voice behind her.

"Brittany, this is nonsense. Why would Scotty's uncle want to meet with you? This is getting out of hand, don't you think?" He voiced his concern loudly and then turned on his heel and left her standing in shock.

This was so unlike Blake, but she forced herself not to go after him. *He needs to get a grip on his emotions. I will not accept these types of childish outburst from him. He needs to be aware of this. Maybe that's the reason I didn't tell him the entire truth. He's being so foolish.*

Blake questioned himself. What was getting into him? He shouldn't have acted that way. If he could remember where she had said she was meeting the uncle, he would go and apologize. But wait, she had NOT told him where they were going. Growing agitated, he wondered if she had purposely not told him. Everything seemed to be going all wrong since that little boy entered their lives. She hadn't even mentioned their wedding plans in the last couple of weeks. Surely she wasn't so preoccupied with that kid that she had forgotten she was getting married to him? He slammed his fist in anger on his desk.

Meanwhile Adam was ingratiating himself with Brittany. He leaned toward her and spoke earnestly. "Please, let me begin by apologizing again for my actions at the hospital the other day. I am very sorry if I embarrassed you. I'll have to explain my reaction by starting at the beginning – that means the first time I ever saw you."

Brittany could not believe what a nice time she was having with Adam. She also was enjoying his awkwardness in trying to explain his behavior. Sipping her wine, she lowered her eyes and continued to pretend she had been offended by his actions.

"It all started quite some time ago," he began. He fiddled with the napkin nervously. "You see, I had seen you a while back when I rented a cabin in the mountains for the weekend. I saw you there with a man."

Now Brittany looked up at him with a small frown.

"When...? With Blake, of course."

"Yes, I realize that the man is Blake Daniels, whom I spoke to briefly in the cafeteria." He gave a sheepish smile as he admitted, "Anyway, I thought you were so beautiful that your face took up residence in my mind. The first day I arrived back here, I walked into the courtroom and there you were. You can't imagine how shocked I was to see you. And then to see you again at the hospital, and working there .... Wow!" He shook his head and continued as she stared into his eyes. "I hope you really can forgive me for acting like such a jerk. I'm not that person at all. What made my actions even worse was to find out that you're the special friend Scotty spoke so highly of."

She smiled softly at Adam and extended her hand to him. "There's no need to apologize again. Honestly. We all have our bad moments. Besides, that patient and I had a little chuckle over the way you acted. Really, it's okay."

If only he knew what she had been thinking the first time she had laid eyes on him, she would be the one begging for forgiveness. Of course she would never tell him, even though she had the odd feeling she wanted to.

During the evening, they shared stories about Scotty. Adam confided   he had worried if Scotty was getting the attention he needed from his parents, never realizing they were also harming him. He told her he was happy to have the opportunity to raise Scotty. "

In turn, Brittany shared the fact that Scotty had filled an empty space in her life that she didn't even know existed. She cared very much for Scotty and was happy he had Adam, rather than strangers. "If I had been in your situation, Adam, I know I would be doing the same as you."

46

She wanted to know more about this man who would change his entire life for his nephew. Brittany had a feeling she would receive this chance.

Looking at her intently, Adam propped his arm on the table and rested his chin in the palm of his hand. "Can I ask you sort of a personal question?" he asked.

Brittany was pleased. Just as she wanted to know things about him, he also wanted to know about her. She smiled coyly at him. "Sure, I don't mind." Her pulse quickened at the thought that if she answered a question of his, he would surely answer one of hers.

"The man I saw you with, Blake Daniels, at the cabin," he began as he released his chin and straightened his back, "do you see him still?"

His question took her by surprise. How well did he know Blake? She leaned back in her chair and cleared her throat, "How did you know it was Blake Daniels ?"

Brittany watched as his shoulders seemed to relax.

"Well, as I mentioned briefly before, I ran into him at the hospital and immediately recognized him as the man I had seen you with at the cabin. I did, however, in the short conversation we had, find out he is not married to you." Adam leaned forward and touched her hand "I must say I was relieved to hear that. I still wondered if you two were in any type of relationship."

Brittany thought he wasn't too subtly trying to find out if she had any strong relationship with Blake, even though he tried to act as if his actions and speech belied his concern. Shrugging his shoulders, he curled his lips slightly. "I thought it best not to ask too many questions."

47

When she allowed his hand to linger on hers, she inadvertantly stroked his hand with her thumb. With eyes lowered, she confided softly, "I had begun to work on plans for my wedding to Blake when Scotty came into my life. Then, I kind of put our wedding on the back burner to be with and help Scotty."

Suddenly realizing they were nearly holding hands, she slid her hand away from his. "I think," she continued, "that I have upset Blake tremendously by doing so."

Nervously, she lifted her glass and swallowed another sip of red wine. "I wasn't trying to upset him, it's just that helping Scotty made me feel as if I was doing a good thing. It made me feel whole somehow."

When he made no comment, she put down her glass and shifted about in her chair. Adam heard her whisper, "I've known Blake my entire life and he's a wonderful person."

Adam's eyes held hers as she admitted so softly as if she were talking to herself, "Lately, he's been acting so different, and I believe it has everything to do with Scotty. I don't really seem to know Blake at all."

Adam flashed her a smile when she looked up at him. " I just know Blake is a very lucky man."

As Brittany lay in bed trying to read, she could hardly concentrate on her book. Her thoughts kept going back to her dinner with Adam -- remembering his smile and the way he had looked at her. She allowed herself to fantasize what it would be like to be held and kissed by him until she was jolted back into reality by the ringing of her phone.

When she glimpsed her caller ID, she saw Blake's number. Answering the call, she nearly called him Adam. Brittany drew in her breath, knowing that would have been a disaster. She was dismayed and could not understand what had come over her. *I love Blake. I know I do. Why am I thinking of another man?*

Adam was convinced he had seen something in Brittany's eyes that told him she wasn't completely happy. If she had been so anxious to marry Blake Daniels, then nothing would have stood in the way of their wedding plans – not even concern for a child. Scotty was a good excuse for Brittany, but he wasn't buying it. Something else was wrong in that relationship, and he vowed he would find out what it was.

Running his hand through his hair, Adam felt very selfish when he admitted to himself that he hoped Brittany would never finish planning for the wedding. He felt she wasn't right for Blake, but that could be because he wanted Brittany to be right for him.

Chapter 9

Blake had been taking a walk when he saw Brittany get out of Adam's car. She was supposed to be with Scotty and his uncle. So why was she with Adam Franklin? And why had she lied to him? When he called her later that evening, she had sounded somewhat distant, yet she told him everything was fine. He had even asked how the evening had gone with the uncle and she had responded that things had gone well.

Brittany inhaled the sweet aroma of the dozen long-stem yellow roses she had received today. The card had simply read, "Brittany" which left a question in her mind as to who had sent them. Blake had been a little too distant to suddenly send flowers. This left only Adam.

He probably sent me flowers as a thank you. Instanly, she retracted that thought. *Of course, they must be a peace offering from Blake. How silly of me to think Adam would send me flowers!*

Blake had run into Adam several times during the day. Being so busy, Adam had not noticed the strange looks he was getting from Blake. Vowing he would do anything to keep Brittany, Blake decided to keep an eye on the good doctor Adam. A little later he observed Adam and Brittany standing together laughing in the hallway. *What has Adam said to make her laugh that way?* It was hard to remember the last time he himself had made her laugh.

Brittany was showing Adam a piece of paper with

hearts drawn all over it. "This is the sweetest letter I have ever received. He's asking me to be his girlfriend. Isn't this so sweet? And look how he carefully colored in each heart."

Adam had to admit his nephew had a lot more courage than he did. "Well, Scotty told me he wanted you to have the letter right away. He is surely a smart boy who knows a good thing when he sees it."

When Adam suddenly stopped smiling, Brittany turned to see what had caused his abrupt change and spied Blake standing nearby, glaring at them with the most peculiar look on his face. She glanced back at Adam as she called out Blake's name, but Blake only walked away.

The next few hours were uneventful, but she brooded about Blake when she had a moment to think. She checked in on patients and even took time to sit and chat with a couple. When she saw Blake down the corridor, she rushed to catch up with him. "Blake, why didn't you answer me earlier when I called your name? I know you heard me. Why did you just walk away like that?"

Sarcastically, Blake answered, " I didn't want to interrupt the wonderful time you were having with Dr. Franklin." Blake disregarded any hurt his answer would cause Brittany.

Brittany reached into to her pocket and pulled out the letter Scotty had given her and held it up. "Scotty had him deliver this cute little letter to me.

"Now what does Dr. Franklin have to do with Scotty?" Blake was annoyed.

"Blake, don't you know that Adam Franklin is Scotty's uncle? He dropped everything in his life and moved back here just to care for Scotty."

By the look on Blake's face, Brittany knew she had said those words a little too boldly. Blake felt his anger rise. "As a matter of fact, I did NOT know that! You failed to mention that fact before!"

Brittany felt this was not sounding good! He knew how much Scotty meant to her, but he wasn't going to give up so easily. He already didn't like the idea of her spending so much time with the boy.

Blake felt fury run through his veins at the thought she had spent any time with Adam Franklin! Yet, he tried to smile and sound calm, but his voice sounded sarcastic. "Well, I guess this is a comfort to you and all of us. Now we know for sure that Scotty is in good hands, even better than we could have imagined. Not only is his uncle willing to care for him, but he's also a doctor Now maybe we can get on with our lives. Right, darling?"

Brittany noticed the smug look on Blake's face and decided she was not going to back down. Approaching him, she pursed her lips and said in a steady, strong voice, "Our lives never stopped. As a matter of fact, Blake, mine has been enriched by Scotty. It feels good to know I am helping a child heal."

Undaunted, Blake placed his hands on Brittany's shoulders and said in a cajoling voice, "Well, of course you helped him. But now his uncle is here, and you can back out and no longer worry about Scotty."

Brittany shrugged off his hands and retorted loudly, "I don't want to back out. That child needs me. He needs anyone who can show him kindness and love. Why can't you understand that? Scotty had a traumatic thing happen to him that will scar him mentally for life. He lost his parents, for God's sake, Blake! Have a little sympathy here! Stop being so self-

52

ish!"

She turned to walk away, but Blake grabbed her arm. "I have been sympathetic," he said through gritted teeth! "I'm not going to sit back and watch you help raise Scotty with Adam Franklin! There's something I don't like about this, and it's the idea of your being with Adam!"

She jerked her arm free from Blake. "You know what I think your problem is, Blake? I think you're jealous! Jealous that I have interests other than you. You've been acting very odd lately, and I'm not so sure I like that. Now if you will excuse me, I have work to do!"

"Oh, that's what you think this whole thing is about? Jealousy? Well perhaps you should think again! I'm thinking of us! Remember us? Tell me, when was the last time you worked on our wedding plans? Or have you forgotten that we are to be married?"

She was so furious she could feel her blood boiling. "How could I forget that!" she snapped! "That's the only thing you make sure I do remember! I'm very aware that we're engaged." She held her left hand inches from his face. "This engagement ring is a symbol of love, not ownership! I wear it to let the world know I love you. We haven't even set an actual date, so it's not like I have a deadline to meet. All I have been trying to do is help a little boy. Certainly our love is strong enough to sustain that. If not, then we have a terrible problem at hand here."

Brittany's body tembled. She had never had such a heated argument with anyone, especially Blake.

Seeing her so shaken and upset, he forced himself to calm down. Taking her trembling hands in his, he spoke. "It's not jealousy. I just thought our getting married was the most

53

important thing in the world for you. It certainly is to me. I'm glad you were able to help a child. But he's in good hands now. Being helpful to Scotty was fine, but making yourself so available to his uncle may not be such a good idea. He could get the wrong idea."

She shook her head in disbelief. "Why are you so eager to jump to the wrong conclusion? If you would take the time to get to know Adam better, you would see that he has Scotty's best interests at heart. You are always welcome to come along with me when I go to see Scotty. You've known that from the start, but you chose not to participate. Scotty is a real joy, especially at the end of a long day. You should at least try. He'll even make you laugh."

At first, Blake was shocked by her vehemence. Then he reacted by listening intently. Now he surprised her by kissing her forehead gently. "We'll see. I have to get going. Do you have any plans for dinner tomorrow night?"

She almost hesitated to answer his question. "Tomorrow the Judge gives the final okay on Scotty's staying with Adam. I'm sure Scotty will want me to celebrate with Adam and him. If so, won't you please join us? I would love it if you would. We would ALL love it."

Blake controlled the resentment he began to feel at that very moment. Giving a faint smile and a quick
kiss to her cheek, he left.

Chapter 10

Scotty was allowed to enter the courtroom with his uncle by his side. He knew that in a few minutes he would belong to his uncle and would always get to live with him. At times, he still missed having a mommy and daddy. He had always tried to be a good boy when he had lived with his parents, but he couldn't understand why he had always been yelled at for any reason.

Uncle Adam never raised his voice at him or treated him unkindly. Brittany and Uncle Adam were the nicest people in the world. He really hoped one day that Brittany would live with them so they could be a family.

Brittany joined Adam in the courtroom, glad to share this moment with them. Yet, her mind kept drifting back to Blake and his strange behavior. While lying in bed last night, she had actually questioned herself whether she had been neglecting Blake. She had almost begun to feel guilty. *But why? I shouldn't feel guilty fo helping Scotty and wanting to be friends with his uncle. I know Adam wants to fall in love and find someone who would be a real mother to Scotty. But he surely knows I'm not that person. He's well aware of my engagement to Blake.*

Her thoughts were disrupted by the feel of Adam's arm around my shoulder. This brought their bodies closer and made her feel just a little uncomfortable. She wanted to move away, but didn't want to upset the good mood that filled the room at that time.

Blake quietly entered the courtroom, wanting to be there for Brittany in case something went wrong. He did feel bad about the disagreements they had been having and thought this was the place to start fresh. He would show her that he really did care and understood how much the boy meant to her. But when he spotted them, he saw Adam and Brittany sitting together in the second row. Adam's arm was around her, and they were sitting too close. They looked like any other ordinary couple waiting to adopt a child. His body ached with a pain he could not describe as he felt his heart dissolve inside his chest. He couldn't face her now, and left the courtroom as quietly as he had entered.

When all discussions and rulings were out of the way, Scotty was now Adam's. When the Judge gave the final word, Scotty gave Adam a high five. Adam hugged Brittany tightly and gave her a peck on the lips. She was so happy, but his slight kiss fogged her mind. Had he been wanting to do that or had he just lost himself in the moment?

Scotty was happy and felt very lucky, but at the same time he felt a sadness overwhelm him. "Will I ever get to see them again?" His eyes were clouded with tears as he looked at Adam. Adam picked him up and held him in his arms. He knew in the beginning that he would some day have to answer this question. "Yes, Scotty, you will see them again. They have what is called visitation rights. First, they have to take a parenting class, and when they have finished and passed that class, they will be allowed to visit you. Their visits will take place in our home once a month. I'll always be there. I promise."

Brittany felt tears begin to fill her own eyes. She reached over and caressed Scotty's hair in a loving manner. Scott smiled shyly at her, then turned to ask his uncle another question. "What about Brittany? Can she live with us too? You said you wanted a nice family. You, me and Brittany can be family."

Surprised by Scotty's words, Adam and Brittany looked at each other with puzzled expressions. Brittany spoke first. "Scotty, honey, I can't live with you and Adam, but I can spend time with you. Just like I always have." With those words she realized she had just committed more time to Scotty. *What else could I have said? I did mean this, after all, but it is certain to upset Blake.*

By the look in Brittany's eyes, Adam suspected she was a little uneasy about telling Scotty she would spend more time with him. His instincts told him her uneasiness had a lot to do with Blake Daniels. He decided to change the subject. "Well, with all that has happened today, I'm now pretty hungry. How about anyone else? We could go to that little hamburger place on the corner and get a bite to eat there. What do you two say?"

Adam saw the hesitation in Brittany's eyes. He didn't want her to feel as if he was pushing her to do something she didn't want to do, but he wanted her near him. Anxiously he waited for her response, while she suddenly decided she had to get away. *I really need to get going. I'll pick up a few items from the grocery store. Then I need to get in touch with Blake.*

When Adam perceived she would tell him *no*, he thought he would give it one more try. "This celebration won't be the same without you, Brittany."

Brittany did not want to let them down. This WAS a celebration of some kind. She smiled at them both and said gently, "Okay, but right after we eat, I have to be going." Anyone passing the three of them on the street would have thought they were a happy family.

Later, Brittany sat at her dining table going through
57

her mail. Knowing Blake would be busy at the hospital yet, she would not call him, but she had begun to miss him. She had so much wanted to share this happy day with him. *Why couldn't he have just shown up? I didn't mean to hurt him. I have to let him see that somehow. I just wanted him to share how I felt about Scotty. Tonight I'll make him a nice dinner. Then we could attend a movie and have a romantic evening together.*

She'd have to hurry. She didn't have much time. After putting away the mail, she began to make a tossed salad. Then she placed a large, boneless chicken breast in a baking dish, poured her home-made Italian red sauce over it, added mozzarella cheese, and placed it in the oven. She looked at the long loaf of crusty Italian bread and set that aside on a pan to warm up later. Taking a deep breath, she stepped back and allowed the aroma of the food to feed her senses.

Something was missing. *Flowers. I need flowers.* Hurriedly she ran downstairs to the florist next door and purchased bright yellow marigolds.

There now. With the marigolds and lighted candles as a centerpiece, the setting is now perfect.

She sat down to wait.

Blake always stops by to see me before going home. But it's already thirty minutes past his normal arrival time. Maybe he thinks I would still be with Scotty and Adam. I'll call him to tell him I'm home.

Brittany picked up the phone and dialed Blake's number.

Blake wished the phone would stop ringing! How many times would a person let the phone ring before giving up? He couldn't stand it much more, but would show her by not answering. *I, Blake Daniels play second fiddle to no one.*

He hadn't been able to put the picture of her and Adam sitting together in that courtroom out of his head. They were a perfect picture of a perfect couple. *No, I'm not going to answer her phone call. I have to make her miss me. Only then will she realize that being with me is more important than being with that boy and his uncle!* It wasn't easy not to answer her calls. He did love her but he was not giving in.

Brittany was beginning to worry. In the past, Blake had always phoned her if he was staying late at the hospital. Anxious now, she pressed the hospital's number on her phone and spoke to one of the nurses. The nurse told her he had left at his usual time. She also told Brittany he had kept to himself all afternoon after he returned from the courthouse, speaking only when absolutely necessary.
Brittany thanked the nurse and ended the call.

So he had come to the courthouse. Why hadn't he let me know he was there and why hadn't he stayed? She tried thinking of a reason he would do such a thing. When nothing came to mind, she decided she would drive to his apartment if he didn't show up this evening.

Chapter 11

"Blake, Blake! Good morning. Where were you last night? I waited for you to come by after work or at least call me. I called you several times. I even drove to your place last night and you didn't answer your door. And why didn't you let me know that you had showed up at the courthouse yesterday?" Brittany knew she was firing questions at him, but she had had little sleep. She had stayed up most of the night pacing and worrying about him.

She detected a nasty sarcasm in his voice when he held up his hand and answered, "Before you go on with your questioning, let me remind you that you said you would be celebrating with Scotty and Adam."

Brittany didn't understand his attitude. He had been invited to join them. It had been his choice not to come along.

Frowning, he continued, "Brittany what do you expect from me? You want me to just wait around until you're finished with those two? It's just not that way. Not now, not ever!" He put out his hands for emphasis.

"But Blake," she began and was interrupted by Adam

himself.

"Good morning, you two. Brittany, have you told Blake the good news yet?"

Before Brittany could say another word, Blake turned on his heels and walked out the door.

"Blake, please wait," she called after him. He kept on walking.

Adam touched Brittany's arm. "Let him go," he said. Let him be alone and cool down. It's the best thing to do right now."

"But Adam...oh maybe you're right," she grumbled. "He's been acting so strangely lately. Slowly, he's building a wall between us. Blake doesn't like, or never did like my spending so much time with Scotty. Now that you've entered the picture, it's only gotten worse. I just wanted him to understand that Scotty is just a little boy in need of a lot of affection right now."

Adam could see exactly what the problem was. "Yes, but Brittany, I'M not a little boy," he said. He held both her hands now and looked into her eyes. "You say he's been acting worse since I came into the picture. Then it must be me. I can understand that If you were mine, I would be cautious of whom you spent your time with too."

Brittany disengaged her hands. "Don't be silly, Adam. Blake knows I love him. My goodness, we've been together forever. I'm planning our wedding."

Of course what Adam had said to her had crossed her mind. She just couldn't understand all of this anger or whatever it was coming from Blake. He had always been such a level-headed guy, and now he was everything but. *Perhaps I should have gone after Blake anyway, instead of listening to Adam. What do I really expect to get out of this relationship with Scotty and Adam? It seems that Adam knows that Blake is jealous of him.*

61

Adam did know that Blake was jealous of him and if he himself were honest with Brittany he would tell her that Blake had every right to be. Adam realized he was falling in love with her and was giving it his best shot to make her fall in love with him. *I really believe she feels something for me. too. I won't push her, though. She just hasn't realized it yet and will figure it out on her own, I'm sure.*

Blake was livid. Couldn't Brittany see that Adam was trying to tear them apart? And he was using her feelings for Scotty to do so. Adam knew the boy was the way to her heart. He saw the way Adam looked at her and hated the thought of her being anywhere near him. Right now he wished that he and participated more in the things she had been doing with Scotty. He had to get rid of Adam somehow.

The next day proved to be a rough day for Brittany. No matter how hard she tried, she couldn't seem to focus on her work. She felt so torn between Blake and Scotty. Maybe Blake was right. Adam was here, and she didn't have to be so involved in Scotty's life. It would break her heart not to see Scotty so often, though, and she prayed he would understand. Her thoughts swirled in a jumble of confusion. *But maybe it would be best if I do back off. It's breaking my heart to hurt Blake, too.*

Not long after she arrived home that evening, the phone rang. When she saw it was Adam's number, she wrestled with the decision about whether to answer or not. After a long hesitation, she picked up the phone, only to hear Scotty's sweet voice asking her if she would come with him and Adam to the petting zoo.

"Scotty, that sounds like a lot of fun," she answered softly, but I don't think I can today. With a lump in her throat and tears in her eyes, she talked a little more and finally said
62

goodbye to him.

So this was how backing off from Scotty was going to feel. She felt an overwhelming emptiness and needed to be comforted. Picking up the phone again, she punched in Blake's number. There was no answer.

Blake watched Adam and Scotty load the red sports car. They had a cooler and a picnic basket -- all the essentials for a nice little get-together.

"They aren't going to get away with this one," he said aloud as he slammed his car door shut!

As Adam and Scotty got into their car and began to drive, he followed. He stayed with them for a distance and realized they had passed Brittany's exit to her apartment.

"She must be meeting them somewhere," he mumbled to himself. He continued to follow them, keeping out of sight until they reached their destination. They exited the car, but he didn't see Brittany anywhere. It didn't look as if they were looking for her either. He followed them on foot as far as he could without having to pay for admission to the zoo. Being careful, he once more searched for Brittany. He waited and watched. Still no Brittany. Adam was with Scotty on this outing alone. Relieved, Blake returned to his car and called Brittany.

"Blake. I tried to call you," Brittany said trying to sound more cheerful than she actually felt.

"I'm sorry, Brittany, but I had errands to run," he lied. "How about going for a bite to eat? Your choice."
out
Brittany agreed to go with Blake and placed her phone on the table. When she entered her bedroom and opened the closet door, she stared fixedly at her clothes. Suddenly

63

they all seemed old and tired. She needed something new, something exciting. She made a mental note to make time for herself to go on a shopping spree.

Blake was still curious about why Brittany had not joined Adam and Scotty at the zoo. "Where's Scotty and his uncle?" he asked, knowing full well where they were.

Brittany knew there was ridicule in his question and it changed her mood. "I believe they went to the petting zoo," she answered in an acid tone. Now agitated, she added, "I was invited, but I turned down the invitation."

Blake felt smug. *Just maybe the other night had taught Brittany something after all. Now she knows I don't just exist to wait around for her. But, of course, that's not true. I would wait forever, as I've always done, but I don't see the reason for reminding her of that right now. Now's the time to play hardball. If Dr. Adam hasn't realized that Brittany belongs to me, he soon will.*

Somehow, Brittany sensed Blake's cocky attitude and didn't like it. "Blake, I feel like these days I am constantly repeating myself when it comes to Scotty. As I've said many times before, I was only trying to help a needy child." She shook her head hopelessly and crossed her arms over her chest, glaring at him. "There's nothing wrong with showing a little boy some much-needed attention and love."

He shot her a bitter glance. "Brittany, I, too, feel as if I'm repeating myself. All I am saying is give his good 'ole uncle a chance to show the boy those things. You've done the right thing. Now, allow him to take over."

Blake sounded so arrogant that Brittany couldn't hold back her own sarcasm. "Why Blake, that's the only reason I turned down the invitation to the zoo. I thought it would be
64

best if Adam had time alone with Scotty."

She watched as Blake's face turned white and then red. She knew her answer had unsettled him, but she felt he had deserved that answer.

Deserved or not, she saw a shocked surprise on his face. Rage seared his veins as he tried hard not to show his anger. Her answer should have been that she turned it down to be with him! What was wrong here? He was going to have to have a word with the good doctor Adam tomorrow. He hated the way Adam's name slid over her lips. She made it sound like Aaadam, drawing out the beginning of his name. He wanted her to call him Dr. Franklin, not Adam. He would bring this up to her tomorrow. *It's improper to call him anything but Dr. Franklin.*

Brittany felt the evening turning into a disaster. Feigning a yawn, she covered her mouth and said, "Why don't we call it a night? I feel quite over-tired suddenly."

Blake wasn't ready to be separated from her just yet. "I'm sorry you're not up to a longer evening out. Maybe we could go to my place and watch a movie."

"I'm afraid not this time, Blake." She gathered her purse and placed it across her shoulder. "I think I'm just going to go home and relax with a book. I'm sure I'll fall asleep quickly."

Brittany was glad to be home and away from Blake's sarcastic remarks. A quiet evening at home would be exactly what she needed.After seeing Brittany safely inside her apartment, Blake began his drive home. His emotions were so out of control that he couldn't think straight any longer. He was so distraught by their relationship. If Adam thought for one minute that he was going to sit back and let him steal Brittany, he'd better think again! As he sped down the highway, he de-
65

cided something had to be done to end the relationship.

Brittany poured a glass of soda and snuggled up on the sofa with her book. She kept reading the same sentence over and over. The book couldn't seem to hold her interest, and before long she dozed off into a restless sleep.
The buzzing of her cell phone startled her from her dream. Still groggy, she answered her phone and was surprised to hear Scotty's voice on the other end.

Before she could even finish the word hello, Scotty was already speaking excitedly. "Brittany, I wanted to tell you something."

Still not quite awake, Brittany interrupted him. "Is everything okay, Scotty? Where's Uncle Adam?"

She then heard a giggle come through the phone. "He's right here, Brittany. I just want to tell you about the petting zoo."

Glimpsing the clock on the wall, Brittany saw that it was only eight p.m. She felt as if she had been sleeping much longer than she actually had. Her mind drifted back to only moments before, and she realized she had been dreaming of Adam.

"Brittany," she heard Scotty's small voice again.

Her mind still cloudy, she answered, "Yes, honey, I'm here. Could you hold on for just one minute, please?" She needed to take a second and gather herself. As she put the phone down, she heard his faint, "Yeah."

A full ten seconds passed until she picked up her phone again and began to speak. "Okay, Scotty, I'm
sorry. I was just...."
66

She was interrupted by Adam's voice. "Scotty handed me the phone. He said you sounded sick or something. Is everything okay?"

She decided that everything was fine except that she might possibly die of embarrassment. "Oh, I was reading a book and must have fallen asleep. I think I was still half asleep when I answered the phone."

"Okay, then," Adam said smiling to himself as he visualized her beautiful face fresh from a nap. "I think he's about to burst open standing here. He loved the zoo so much. Shall I put him back on?"

"Yes, please do."

Adam handed the phone to Scotty. " I wanted to tell you how much fun the zoo was. I petted a monkey! A real one!" He continued telling her about his day and all the different animals he had encountered.

She loved that his voice was so filled with cheer. Brittany, herself, was full of smiles after talking to Scotty. What a joy to have him in her life.

Her thoughts drifted back to Blake and then to her dream of Adam. Subconsciously, she began to compare the two. Adam was very pleasant, and so had Blake been until a few weeks ago. Adam was certainly being responsible in stepping up to take care of his nephew. How many men would take on the responsibility of caring for their sister's child? She considered that Blake also was usually kind and probably would have done the same if he had a nephew that needed him. Both men were also very good looking.

"Ugh," she said aloud. She didn't want to be doing this. Under no circumstances should she be thinking of Adam.

She should be concentrating on her wedding plans. And she would. Tomorrow, right after work.

With that thought, she curled into bed, falling asleep within minutes and dreamed of Adam.

Chapter 12

The next morning, Brittany awoke feeling refreshed. Stepping into the shower, letting the warm water massage her body, she closed her eyes, only to be reminded of her latest dream of Adam. How warm in her dreams she had felt lying next to him. She snapped her eyes open and scolded herself. Forget those dreams!

Blake was waiting for her at the nurse's station when she arrived for work. "I want to apologize for last night. I really acted like a jack ass. I love you. I'm sorry." He nervously cracked his knuckles as he waited for her reaction.
She was not prepared for this or anything Blake had to say today, but she certainly wasn't in the mood to fight, either.

"Blake, it's okay. Maybe you have a right to be upset. I don't know. Tonight I'm getting back to work on our wedding plans. Now I had better see to my patients."

He agreed with a boyish wink as Brittany hurried on to her first patient. She was glad to see Blake headed in the opposite direction. Guilty. She felt so guilty about her dreams, and she knew that was the reason she had let him off the hook so easily. She tried to make herself feel better by thinking about her wedding plans, but somehow Adam's face crept into her mind.

Blake was riding high on his ego. He was proud of his accomplishment, sure that avoiding Brittany the other night had been the right thing to do. She wasn't even mad at him for acting like a jerk and was beginning to work on their wedding plans again. *No one is going to take Brittany from me! Especially the good Doctor Adam. And now I will show her just how charming I can be to a young child. Yes, now is the time to step into the spotlight.*

Brittany's morning only worsened when she heard a couple of the other nurses talking. They were remarking how they'd like to get their hooks into Adam and were curious about what it would take to get him. That's when she heard her name being mentioned.

"You know, she and Adam are an item. Gossip has it that they are secretly seeing each other and it is just a matter of time before Blake finds out."

She stood frozen. "How can they think that of me? My interest is in Scotty, not Adam!" She slid into a vacant room to keep from being noticed. She had to keep remember that this was only gossip. But it would do her no good for Blake to get wind of this sort of talk. *Perhaps that had already happened. That would explain his recent actions. People are always saying how hospitals are like soap operas. Well, I'm not going to stand by while they make one of my life. I'll put a stop to this immediately!*

Suddenly, she was sartled to hear Adam's voice. She dropped her clipboard as she heard him say, "Brittany, have you taken the patient's vitals in 304 yet?"

A passing nurse giggled at the scene taking place. Out of concern, Adam placed a hand on Brittany's shoulder. "A little jumpy today, are we?"

She bent and picked up her clipboard, grateful that his

hand slid off her shoulder. The heat she felt from his touch subsided instantly. "I'm sorry, Adam. My mind was elsewhere for a minute."

She hoped he had not actually caught her eavesdropping on her coworkers. She straightened up and declared, "Mrs. Archer is coming along fine. I really believe she could even be released today."

"Great, I'll go in and check on her now and if she's as good as you say, I'll get the release papers in order." As he looked at Brittany, he slanted his head and gave a litle frown. "Are you okay? You look like *you're* the one that needs a doctor."

When she gasped, he realized how his words must have sounded, and he cleared his throat before saying, "I mean, maybe you should see the doctor that takes care of you when you're not well."

She felt somewhat embarrassed by his words. "No, really, I'm fine. I was deep in thought when you approached me." She shifted her her weight to one side. "By the way, you haven't heard any rumors lately, have you?"

Adam laughed. "This is a hospital. Of course I hear rumors every day, nearly every minute. Anything in particular I should know about?"

She backed away, even more flustered than before. "I guess that was a silly question. Of course you hear rumors. We all do. I had better finish my rounds." Without another word, Brittany disappeared into the next room.

Something has surely spooked her, thought Adam. *Her mind was definitely on something other that work. Or some-*

71

one. *Rumors. What has she heard? No one really pays any attention to anything said around here.* He made a mental note to keep his ears open and try to find out exactly what was bothering her. He realized he he had not had the chance to ask her to lunch as he had planned.

Brittany could hardly wait for the morning to end. Five more minutes and she would go to lunch. *I hope Blake is not in one of his moods. I want more than anything to take this next hour to unwind. Right now, though, I feel the need to be held by Blake and feel his kiss. At this very moment, I need him.*

As soon as she had finished with her last patient, she almost ran to the cafeteria where she had agreed to meet Blake. Entering it, she allowed her eyes to search for him, but she did not see him. Suddenly, she spotted Blake and Adam together, entering the cafeteria at the same time. She hunkered down into one of the chairs and tried to be invisible to them, but Blake saw her and pointed her out to Adam. Chatting like old buddies, they strolled over to the table and sat down.

Brittany was confused by this new revelation of friendship. From the look on Adam's face, he seemed just as confused as she felt. After a few moments, she found herself seated next to Blake, who kept talking right along.

"So, Adam," Blake was saying, "Brittany and I would like to take young Scotty to the movies tonight." Pausing for a second, he looked in her direction. "Wouldn't we, honey?" She was more confused than ever. They had not had any type of discussion on taking Scotty to the movies, or anywhere. "Well...we..what?" she asked, in need of an explanation.

Blake reached over and patted her hand with his. "The movies, honey," he said as if she should know what he was

72

talking about. "Adam could use a little break, I'm sure. He's been entertaining Scotty every evening. This will give him an opportunity to catch up on some reading or have a quiet evening to himself. Maybe he could even take a date to dinner. Every man needs to have time alone with a woman. Don't you agree, Adam?"

Adam tilted his head back to take short quick swallows of the bottle of water he was holding tightly in his hand. "We'll, yes, Blake, I agree. But let me get used to one thing at a time. Most men get used to a marriage before the child comes along. With me it's happened just the opposite. I don't feel the need to 'mommy shop' shall I say." Taking one last swallow of his water, he directed a smug smile towards Blake.

Brittany knew Blake was up to something, but she hadn't quite figured it out yet. "Blake, I would love to take Scotty to the movies tonight, but I was planning on working on our wedding plans. Perhaps, though, after the movies you could come over and we could work on things together. Wouldn't that be nice?" Having made her point, Brittany flagged down a cafeteria volunteer and ordered a diet cola.

"I could do that," Blake said, sounding very sure of himself. "I'd rather have you join us because I don't want Scotty to be uncomfortable. He's only seen me, what, once or twice ? The movie should end early enough for us to still work on the wedding."

He turned to Adam. "Would six o'clock be okay for us to pick him up?"

Adam crossed his arms over his chest. "It's fine with me. I'm sure Scotty will enjoy it very much." He stood and looked down at Blake as he said, "I'd better be getting along and see if I can be out of here a little early so I can have Scotty ready." He glanced at Brittany. "Thanks guys."

Adam left the cafeteria feeling more puzzled than when he had first run into Blake. He knew Blake had tried to make it sound as if he and Brittany had already discussed taking Scotty to the movies. But their conversation had proven otherwise. He had no idea why the sudden interest in his nephew from Blake. Maybe this was his way of regaining good grounds with Brittany. Or maybe...Blake wasn't such a bad guy after all. Adam was sure there was good in everyone, although some buried it more deeply than others. He had to have good in him somewhere....he had Brittany.

As soon as Adam was out of hearing range, Brittany turned to Blake. "You mind telling me what that was all about?"

Blake stretched out his long legs and crossed them at the ankles. "I've been thinking," he said. "Thinking a lot actually. Scotty does need to know that all grownups aren't monsters. We're a happy, normal couple and I think it would be good for him to see that. He should see that not all grown ups that love each other drink and fight. Right?"

She had to agree that he had a good point. "Thank you, Blake. This so very sweet of you."

Moving closer to rest her hand on his, she willed her mind to slow down, hoping that Blake was doing this for all the right reasons. She knew she shouldn' doubt him, but it was out of the ordinary for him. Maybe the old Blake of not so long ago would have suggested taking a child to a movie, but not this new jealous Blake. She wanted to believe in him again.

Blake took her chin and slanted her face towards his. "I just want you to know that I love you. I just love you, and I want to be a part of all you do."

74

Of course he does. She knew that. Maybe it was just the pressures of life making him overreact lately. Of course he was doing this for Scotty and for her. "And I love you too, Blake Daniels." She reached until her lips met his and she felt the tugging of need inside her come to life.

Blake was thinking how smoothly that had gone as he watched Brittany leave the cafeteria to finish her rounds for the day. Nothing or no one would ever take Brittany from him now. He'd show the boy some extra attention for her. Actually, for himself, he thought as he quietly laughed cynically. This would keep her and the good doctor Adam separated. It would also give Adam a chance to check out some other women. He wouldn't want other women to think Adam was already taken. Especially by Brittany. He had heard the nurses talking. They had had their pretty little heads together gossiping about her and Adam, wondering if Blake Daniels knew how much time the two of them had spent together. He knew all right! And he wasn't about to look like a fool. She was his and his alone! They'd all see. He'd put a stop to their gossip right now!

Adam picked up Scotty up form the sitter early. "Hey, feel up to a movie tonight?" he asked Scotty.

Scotty jumped up and down with excitement. "Yeh, which one?" he exclaimed. "There's the one with the alien that's playing. Is Brittany coming too?"

"Now hold on. Stop jumping for just a second," Adam said playfully. "Brittany is taking you to the movies. Only I'm not going."

When he saw the frown forming on Scotty's face, he added, "Brittany is bringing along her boyfriend. Do you remember Blake?"

"So," Scotty pouted, "why can't you come too? I want you to." The corners of his mouth pointed downwards.

Real or not, this tugged at Adan's heart.
"Come here, little buddy." Adam gently pulled Scotty onto his lap. "I think this would be a good chance for you to get to know Blake a little better." Adam could clearly see that Scotty had no idea why he should know Blake better than he already did. "You see, Blake is Brittany's boyfriend and most likely someday be her husband. So Brittany would like to spend time with the both of you and give you two the chance to be friends, too."

"But I like going places with you and Brittany. You come, too." Scotty pleaded.

"Now, Scotty, everything will be fine. You will have a good time, I promise. Blake is a nice guy. I understand he took your X-rays. Go wash up. They will be here for you soon." He gave his nephew a quick hug. Despite his encouraging smiles, Adam did wish he was going along with them instead of Blake. *In time*, he thought, *in time.*

"Okay, the three of you have a good time," Adam called out from his doorway. He watched as Brittany and Blake walked hand in hand with Scotty down the driveway to Blake's car. "I'll see you around nine or so. Love you, Scotty."

In his mind, he told Brittany he loved her, too, and was shocked at how comfortable he felt admitting this for the first time, even though no one heard him.

That evening, Adam sat on his couch with a new medi-cal book he had been wanting to read. Instead of reading, his mind drifted to thoughts of Brittany. She was smart, beautiful and caring. He wanted her more than he had ever wanted anyone before. Fantasizing about what she would feel
76

like in his arms, he knew she would mold to his form and he would be able to feel her heartbeat against his own. He wanted to feel every inch of her from head to toe and see the desire for him burning in her eyes.

Frustrated, Adam tore his mind away from Brittany. If she married Blake, he would lose her forever. He had no idea how he could stop that from happening, but knew somehow he must. Blake had not fooled him where Scotty was concerned. Blake thought this move of his would stop him from getting any ideas about Brittany. He was a little late for that, since Adam had had ideas about her since the very first time he laid eyes in her at the cabin.

Adam had heard the same rumors that had worried Brittany so much at the hospital. People were speculating about the difficulty of having two lovers working at the same hospital and how clever it was to be using the boy as a cover. He had heard himself mentioned as Brittany's other lover. They couldn't be more wrong. He would never be her "other" lover. He intended to be her only lover!

At the same time, Blake could have thought of fifty other things he would rather be doing. Being with Brittany was great, but he'd enjoy it so much better under different circumstances. Children's movies weren't going to cut it. He'd have to think of some other way to amuse the boy. He wondered how she seemed to be having the time of her life. The only good thing about this was that with every giggle and laugh, she touched him. He gritted his teeth as he wondered if it was this way when she was out with Scotty and Adam. He had to force himself to believe it wasn't.

Chapter 13

With Scotty not feeling well this morning, Adam was running late. He realized Scotty wasn't well enough to go to school, but he also knew the sitter worked mornings. Luckily, he thought of phoning the Brooks, and they said they would be happy to take care of Scotty.

Blake, Brittany and Scotty had all commented on what a great time they had enjoyed at the movies. But Adam couldn't shake the thought that Blake really hadn't had such a good time after all. Still, he had again asked if he could take Scotty out for a few hours the next weekend as well. When Scotty pleaded to go, Adam felt he had to agree, but something about Blake disturbed him. Adam agreed only because Scotty pleaded to go.

Nurse Browning approached Brittany to say roses had arrived for her earlier and she had placed them in the nurses' lounge. For a brief second, Brittany thought of a time not so long ago when she had received similar roses. She excused herself and went to the lounge to find
beautiful long-stem yellow roses. She took a moment to inhale their sweet fragrance and then opened the envelope. Inside was a card that read simply, "Thank you." No sender's name appeared anywhere on the card or envelope. She imagined Blake had probably sent them to thank her for going along with him to the movies with Scott. As she stared blankly at the card, she had another thought. *Perhaps Adam has sent them as a thanks for taking Scotty to the movies.*
78

Great. But if I thank the wrong man that could be very awkward. I'll call the florist to confirm the sender.

As she left the lounge intending to make the call, she bumped right into Adam. He seemed in a cheerful mood. "Good morning. I'm so glad Scotty had a good time with you and Blake. Thanks again."

Brittany noticed he had not mentioned the roses and he had just verbally thanked her. So they probably weren't from him. They had to be from Blake.

As her thoughts swirled, she missed the beginning of what Adam had been saying and heard only ".... nice of the Brooks."

"What? I'm sorry." Her face reddened. "You were saying something about the Brooks?"

"Wow, where did you just go, Brittany?" He appeared to be a bit bothered by her lack of attention. "You haven't heard anything I just said, have you?"

"I'm sorry, Adam." She fixed her focus on him now. "You were saying?"

"The Brooks have Scotty for the day."

Before he could get another word out, she interrupted him. "Oh my, has something happened? Is Scotty okay?"

"Calm down. Geeze, you really were out there somewhere," Adam said softly. "What I said is that Scotty wasn't feeling well this morning, so I had the Brooks look after him today. He had the sniffles and I thought it would be best if he missed school to rest."

She breathed a sigh of relief that Scotty was going to be fine. Now she was sure Blake had been the one to send the roses. Surely Adam would have mentioned them by now.

Adam rushed off when the intercom announced he was needed in the emergency room. *It's just as well,* he told himself, *since Brittany seems to have her mind on something else.* "Again," he muttered under his breath.

"Hi honey," Blake said cheerfully as he rounded the corner and saw her. "How is your morning going?"

Delighted that Blake had been so thoughtful in sending the flowers she answered smiling. "Actually it's been a good morning. Splendid even."

"And why is that?" He hadn't seen her in this good mood in a while. He was curious.

"As if you don't know," she said flirtatiously. "What woman wouldn't love having roses sent to her?" She ran her fingertip up his arm and down his chest, past his stomach and rested it on his belt loop.

Although the sensation of her touching him like that had a strong effect on him, the idea of her receiving roses from someone else was unsettling. But he wouldn't show it.

"What woman wouldn't, Brittany. You got roses this morning?"

"Yes, I did and they are beautiful. I must thank you again later when we are in private." She teasingly kissed him on the lips.

Although he was pleased by her attention, the agitation

80

he was feeling won. "You're welcome. I'm sure. But right now I need to get going. I have an appointment I can't be late for."

Brittany felt more than a little disappointed that he hadn't matched her move. She gave a litle frown, along with a slight smile. "Okay. I love you."

"Roses," he grumbled to himself as he walked to his office. He noticed a couple of the nurses watching him , but he didn't care. He slammed shut his office door, grumbling "Bunch of busy-bodies! Only one other person would send her roses! Good ole doctor Adam!"

Adam hoped the roses hadn't been the reason Brittany had seemed so shaken. He had seen her leaving the nurses' lounge where she had to have seen them. Yet she didn't mention them. "Strange." He was baffled. He hadn't signed his name to the card because he was sure she would realize they were from him. Now he hoped she didn't think they were from Blake. Why would he be thanking her?

Adan began to allow wild images to enter his mind. He had visions of her thanking Blake for the flowers in a special way. She would be dressed in something sexy waiting for Blake to come to her apartment. He hated the thought of Blake touching her and holding her. He couldn't take this much longer.

Brittany went on with her day in a state of confusion as to why Blake had acted so oddly about the roses. She finally decided he hadn't expected them to be delivered so early. She would overlook his reaction, happy only in knowing they were from him and not Adam. Adam sending her roses would have made her uncomfortable. She didn't quite know why, but she thought she would have felt guilty somehow. Maybe it was because her mind seemed to keep going back to her dreams of Adam. She kept remembering how it had felt to be in his strong embrace.

After picking up Scotty from the Brooks' home that afternoon, Adam decided to call Brittany to let her know Scotty was feeling much better. When her voice mail came on after three rings, he left a message. "Hi Brittany. It's Adam. I thought you'd like to know Scotty is feeling better. Call me when you get a minute."

He had seen her leave the hospital earlier. Maybe she was out doing some shopping. He refused to allow his mind to think she was with Blake. But she was.

Blake answered his door on the second ring of the doorbell. "This is quite a surprise." He moved aside to allow Brittany to come in. "What's the occasion?"

She noticed tiny droplets of water still on his body, She was in an amorous mood, and her mind conjured up great scenarios. " I thought maybe you needed some extra attention," she purred. You deserve it and I've missed you. Sometimes we let work and everyday matters drain us and we get so tired. Time starts slipping away, and before we realize it, life has passed us right on by."

She was close enough to him now that she could reach out and touch him, but she refrained. Instead she sidestepped him and put her purse on the couch, but held onto a small bag in her hand.

"Today at work I began thinking about how much time has passed since we made love. It seems so long ago." She smiled provocatively at him,struggling to act like a vixen. She wasn't used to acting out this role, and it felt awkward. She peeked inside the bag she held.

"So I stopped off at the mall on my way over and pur-

82

chased this to help make this night perfect." She held up a receipt. "Oh, now where could my purchase be?" She looked around the room pretending to search for the missing item.

Blake leaned against the wall, enjoying the little game she was playing. His suspicions were already beginning to disintegrate. Who cared about roses and who had sent them anyway? He had the real thing standing right in front of him. And she was freely offering herself to him.

Flirtatiously, she unbuttoned the simple dress she wore. As she let the dress fall to the floor, she revealed her purchase. She stood provocatively in white satin and lace with her hair flowing around her shoulders. Her magnificent body seemed to scream the need for him to caress her.

His eyes soaked in all her beauty. As she stared at him, Blake closed the distance between them in two steps. He drew her close to him and swiftly picked her up. He had missed her and was hungry for her. As his mouth devoured hers, she responded eagerly.

Her hands pulled almost roughly at his hair. Together they rode into the blissful world of intimacy, quietly satisfied in each other's arms after their lovemaking.

Blake was estatic, while Brittany was feeling relief from the guilt of her recent dreams of Adam. "No," she scolded herself, "I mustn't allow my mind to think of that other man. Not here in Blake's arms.

When it was getting dark outside, she decided to go. Blake had fallen asleep, and she didn't want to awaken him. Rising quietly, she wrote a note and left it by his side. It said, "I love you."

When she arrived home, Bfrittany's guilt came rushing

back. Feeling exhausted from all the emotion of the day, she stepped out of the shower and slipped into her long night-gown. On her way to the kitchen, she noticed her answering machine blinking, indicating she had three messages. She kept on walking, telling herself she could listen to them in the morning.

After pouring herself a glass of orange juice, she returned to her bedroom but soon found herself tossing and turning in her bed, disrupting the covers, but unable to fall asleep. Her mind kept bouncing from one subject to another. She began to wonder if Adam had been one of the callers this evening. As she tried to eliminate the thought, she suddenly remembered Scotty had not been feeling well this morning.

She jumped out of bed and stood next to her answering machine. Listening to Adam's voice within seconds, she had a sudden urge to call him. She tried to persuade herself there was no reason to place that call. After all, he had said that Scotty was better. Still, her fingers seemed to have a mind of their own as they pressed his numbers on her phone.

Brittany heard Adam's groggy "hello" almost instantly, as if he had been dozing near the phone. She felt apologetic for waking him.

"Adam," she said in a low voice barely more than a whisper. "It's me, Brittany."

Adam shook his head and rubbed his eyes with the palm of his hand. He spoke quietly, just as she had.

"Hi. Is everything okay? I tried to call you earlier."

"Everything is fine. I only wanted to double check on Scotty." She HAD wanted to check on the child, but deep down she knew she had wanted more to hear his voice.

84

Adam sat straight up and tried to massage a kink out of his neck that he had acquired while sleeping in an awkward position on the couch. He had hoped she would return his calls. "The Brooks told me he had begun to feel better within a couple of hours after I dropped him off this morning. It actually ended up being an enjoyable day for both Scotty and the Brooks."

He knew the answer to his next question, but wanted to hear her reply. "Did you have to stay late at the hospital?" Fearful of her answer, he closed his eyes tightly.

Without warning, Brittany felt weak in her stomach. It shouldn't bother her to admit to Adam that she had spent the evening with Blake. But it did. "No," she answered. "I spent the evening catching up on something I needed to do." Immediately she became angry with herself for her answer. Why hadn't she just been honest with Adam?

"I'm glad that you're okay." He had an answer, and now he wanted to close that subject, terrified she might have something more to add. After speaking for a few moments, they both said goodnight.

Adam hung up the phone, feeling that Brittany had not told him the entire truth. He could hear the slight hesitation in her voice when she answsered his question, which led him to believe she had been with Blake. He didn't want to believe it, but somehow he knew that's where she had been. What puzzled him more was that she still had not mentioned the roses.

Chapter 14

The hospital had been swamped by an onslaught of people admitted with a flu virus that had hit their town pretty hard. With the number of patients she had seen in the last few days, Brittany hadn't had much free time to do anything else. But she had noticed a change in Adam.

Spending the evening with Blake had definitely done good as far as their their relationship was concerned. Brittany believed any fears Blake had been having about her and Adam had diminished or even disappeared. On the other hand, Adam was giving her the cold shoulder, walking around as if he were pouting about something. She just figured that he and Blake had run into one another and had one of their male ego chats. Blake had probably mentioned that they had spent the evening together, and Adam's feelings were probably bruised because she hadn't been totally honest with him about her whereabouts that evening. She nearly felt the need to apologize.

However, today was a beautiful Sunday with the sun shining brightly and the temperature in the low eighties. It was a perfect day to spend at the lake. Brittany had the idea that Blake and she could pick up Scotty and introduce him. to the perfect place to spend the day outdoors.

Picking up her phone, she called Blake to tell him about her idea. His voice came across on his answering machine. Since it was so early, she decided to leave a message and to call later. Meanwhile, she began doing some minor cleaning
86

at her apartment to pass the time. She did wonder where he had gotten off to so early on a weekend morning. She had just begun to scrub the shower when she heard her phone ringing. After rinsing her hands, she answered her phone and heard Blake's voice on the other end. "Brittany, I'm sorry I didn't call you sooner but it was so early when I had to leave and I know how you like to sleep in on the weekends. So I waited until I got here to call."

She was trying to grasp what he was saying, searching her mind for a conversatio, she might have missed. Nothing came to mind. "Blake, slow down. Got where? Where are you?"

Blake was so tired he now realized he hadn't told her where he had gone. "I'm at my parents' house. Mom called around four a.m. to tell me she was on her way to the hospital with Dad."

Brittany had always been fond of Blake's parents. She interrupted while he was speaking. "Oh, Blake I'm sorry. What's wrong? Do you need me to come there?"

Blake took a sip of his very hot, very black coffee. "Dad has had a mild stroke, but we think he is going to be fine. His doctor wants him to stay in the hospital for a few days so he can keep a close eye on him. So I'm going to stay here until the doctor releases him."

She ran her hand through her hair, genuinely saddened by this news. "Please give my love to Robert and Sharon. I'll be more than happy to drive down if you want," she said sincerely.

Her suggestion to come be with him made him smile. "No, I'll be fine.. Thank you though. I'll call you with any updates on what's happening here. And if you talk to Scotty, give him my apologies that we couldn't spend time with him this weekend as promised."

She thought it was very considerate of him to think of Scotty at a time like this. "Okay I will. And it's such a beautiful day here I think I'll go down to the lake."

He wished he was going to the lake with her. The vision of her in her bikini sent thrills up his spine. "Have fun. If you should miss my call, I'll leave a message. I love you."

After ending the call with Blake, she had a decision to make. Should she go alone to the lake or call Adam and ask permission to take Scotty along? She hadn't mentioned to Blake whether she'd be alone or not. Blake might not appreciate her calling Adam while he was out of town. Then again, she was only calling for one simple question. More eager than she should , she called Adam's phone. "Good morning, Adam! Isn't it a beautiful day?" she said with much enthusiasm.

"We'll good morning to you, too." He tried to sound as excited about the day as she did. "Don't you sound chipper! What if anything besides this beautiful weather has you in this great mood?"

She began her reply, "Blake is out of town......"

Adam interrupted her. "Shouldn't that put you in just the opposite..."

Now it was Brittany's turn to interrupt. "You didn't let me finish! I woke up this morning and the sun was shining so brightly that it put me in this wonderful mood. I couldn't think of a better place to spend this day than at the lake." She was determined to not allow Adam to ruin her mood. "And I'm not happy that Blake is out of town. His father suffered a mild stroke and he went to be with him and his mother. He assured
88

me things were going to be fine and that I should enjoy my day. If you'll remember, Blake and I were going to spend time with Scotty this weekend. Obviously Blake can't keep the date, but I can. Would you mind if I pick up Scotty and take him with me?"

Adam was glad she had interrupted him and not allowed him to make light of Blake's absence. He didn't care for Blake, but he certainly didn't wish harm to him or his family.

"I wouldn't mind at all, Brittany." "It would be especially good for him right now. I just had a problem with Scotty's dad, Wes. He showed up here very early this morning demanding to see his son. I wouldn't let him past the front door. He left rather angrily, all the while screaming and cussing about me and my girlfriend. Of course Scotty heard everything. He's upset, and I can understand that. No matter what, Wes is his dad, and I'm sure Scotty misses him and his mom. So, yes, I'd be glad if you did take Scotty out for a little while."

Brittany's heart felt as though it might break. How much more would this little boy have to endure from his parents?

In spite of everything, Brittany's good mood remained, and she decided It had to be the weather and the fact that she was spending time with her favorite little person. When she arrived at Adam's house, she found him raking his front lawn. Getting out of her car, she made the statement, "It is a good day for yard work."

Scotty came running out of the house. "Brittany, Brittany, you're here! Can we go now? I'm ready!"

Kneeling down to his level, she hugged Scotty and spoke with a broad smile. "If you have all your things ready, then we can be on our way,"

Adam stopped raking and watched as Scotty skipped

89

back into the house to gather his things. With a solemn look he turned to face Brittany. "I really appreciate your taking the time to do this today. It will take his mind off sad things." He shook his head and continued, "Things that a little boy should never even have to worry about."

"It will be a lot of fun for the both of us." She walked over to his rose bushes. "This certainly is a very nice yard. Did you do the landscaping yourself? And these roses are just beautiful. You have a bush for each color." She gently held a soft petal between her fingers and brought it to her nose, breathing in the sweet rose fragrance.

Adam thought that now would be the perfect time to ask her the question he had been wanting to ask. "Brittany, I don't mean to sound forward, but mentioning roses, did you get roses at work recently?" There, he had finally asked.

Wondering why Adam would ask such a question, Brittany nonchalantly answered, "Yes, and they were beautiful. I guess Blake is full of all kinds of surprises these days." She smiled sweetly.

"Blake?" He sounded very surprised! "He sent you roses too? Oh boy, I'm sure this really has the nurses' tongues wagging." He chuckled.

Apparently she was missing the funny part of Adam's answer because she wasn't smiling at all. At this point she was thoroughly confused. "What do you mean by 'too?'" She had received roses only once recently, as far as she knew anyway. And she had verbally thanked Blake. They had spent a beautiful evening together inspired by those roses.

The smile disappeared from his face. "The roses you received ... umm ... what did the card say?"

She thought for a second, then replied. "I believe the card simply read, 'Brittany -Thanks.' Why?" She was beginning to feel a little nervous.

"And you thought the roses were from Blake?"

"Yes, I did." She placed her hand on her hip. "Adam, are you saying those roses were from you ?" She didn't know exactly what she was feeling at this moment. Why would Blake let her think he had sent those roses? Why would he deceive her so?

He picked a yellow rose from his rose bush and handed it to her. "Yes, I did. I wanted to thank you for all you have done for Scotty. You've been so kind and helpful."

Her spirits began to sink. Actually she didn't feel well at all. She had made a terrible mistake, and Blake had known all along. Yet, he had allowed her to make a fool of herself.

Adam saw such sadness in her eyes and felt bad for her. He didn't understand why this was upsetting he so. Placing a hand on the back of her arm he asked, "Are you okay? I'm sorry if I've done something that has upset you."

She was determined not to allow this new information to spoil her mood. And she certainly was not going to let Adam know just how upset she actually was. "No, it's just strange. I mean. I wasn't really sure at first who had sent them. Since you didn't mention them when I ran into you coming from the lounge, I assumed Blake had sent them. I even thanked him for them and he didn't deny sending them."

Wow, had she ever thanked him! Her mind went back to the evening of making love.

Scotty stood between them, impatiently waiting for further instructions. He was eager to get going. Adam ruffled Scotty's hair and smiled at him. "You can go ahead and get in the car. Brittany will be right there."

"Okay, but Uncle Adam aren't you coming too? I want to spend the day with you too."

Adam laughed at Scotty's question. "Oh, I don't think that Brittany has any plans of sharing you with me today."

Scotty looked up at Brittany with pleading eyes and his hands clasped together as tightly as he could get them. "Please, please, will you share me today with Uncle Adam? Please."

How could she possibly say no to that sincere little face? And besides she wanted to hear more of what Adam had to say about the roses incident. "That's fine with me if Adam would like to join us." She looked to Adam for an answer.

Adam shrugged his shoulders. "Do you think that's a good idea ? After all. Blake is out of town."

She had her doubts that Blake would be very pleased with her decision to invite Adam, but she wasn't very pleased with Blake right now. She had questions, and just maybe Adam had answers. She grinned a mischievous grin. "I think you should come along, Adam."

Scotty was so excited about going to the lake. He didn't stop talking for the entire drive, talking about school, and his recent day with the Brooks. He made a comment about how his dad had showed up at his house. Scotty was emotionally wounded, no matter how grown-up he tried to act. He was a child, a child who missed his parents. Children have the capability of finding ways to hide behind their
92

true feelings and so far Scotty had done a great job of doing so.

The lake looked so peaceful. It was not as crowded as they had anticipated, so it was fairly easy to find a stretch of grass away from most of the people. Scotty unpacked the toys he had brought along. With permission granted to go play near the water, he took off running.

Once they saw that Scotty was playing peacefully, Brittany turned to Adam. "So...Adam, you were truly the one who sent the roses?"

"Yes, I am. Tell me something, Brittany. What am I missing here?" He sat beside her on the blanket they had carefully spread out on the grass.

Frowning, Brittany replied, "Nothing. As I said before, I thought Blake had sent the roses, that's all. Again, he didn't deny sending them when I thanked him. Brittany looked away from him when she suddenly remembered something Blake had said. "Actually, I just remembered something. I was so nervous about thanking the wrong man. I guess it didn't really register what he was saying at the time. I now recall his answer. He really didn't thank me. All he said was that he was sure the roses were beautiful and he said he was sure I was welcome."

Brittany now felt so foolish and beyond embarrassment . She turned her head, not wanting to face Adam, and fought back tears -- tears that were caused by Blake's deceitfulness.

Adam felt her uneasiness and gently patted her shoulder. "Look, Brittany, I'm sorry about all of this. I never intended the roses to start any kind of trouble. I just wanted to show my gratitude. Do you really think Blake knew all along that I was

93

the one who sent the roses?"

Facing him shyly, she gently answered, "I think he did. He will have some explaining to do when he comes back to town." Her hand touched his. "But thank you for the roses. They were truly beautiful."

He smiled at her warmly and placed his other hand over hers. He wanted to say so much more, but didn't think he had the right. "You're welcome, Brittany."

Brittany looked out at Scotty playing by the water and building sand houses. He had created a small neighborhood with curvy roads by dragging his fingers into the damp sand. He had also used pebbles for cars. Suddenly she had a fun idea. Scrambling to her feet, she smiled at Adam with a devil-ish twinkle in her eyes and yelled, "Let's go play! I'll race you to the water!"

It took only a second for Adam to realize what was hap-pening. In an instant, he was up and chasing Brittany. They were both laughing as they ran towards the water. Just as she reached where Scotty was playing, he caught up with her. She tried to stop but lost her footing, landing in the water head first. Adam grabbed her by the arm and pulled her up. Catching her breath, she slung her head in such a way that her hair sprayed water on Adam and Scotty, getting them wet. She opened her eyes to the look of surprise on both their faces and began laughing.

Adam's quick reflexes had saved her from being com-pletely immersed. And now she was laughing! He gazed at her strangely and then glimpsed at Scotty, whose smile was now turning into a giggle. The whole scenario struck him as funny and, before he knew it , the three of them were laughing uncontrollably.

Scotty began splashing Brittany with water. She shrieked and splashed him back. Adam joined in soaking both of them. It wasn't long before they were completely in the water and their clothes were dripping wet. They were having such a great time they didn't notice the older couple that had stopped to watch them. Nor did they hear their comment. "Isn't it great to see parents so in love with their child? What a nice family."

Finally exhausted from a beautiful day filled with activity, Scotty fell asleep on the way home. Adam carried him to his bed. Immediately upon hitting the bed, Scott curled up to his stuffed bear. With Scotty tucked in bed , Brittany felt it was time to head home. "I had a wonderful day. Adam. I can't remember the last time I had so much fun. Thanks for coming along."

She fidgeted with the keys in her hand while Adam smiled and leaned against the wall. "Thanks for going along with Scotty's unexpected invitation," he said. "I wouldn't have wanted to miss this day for the world." He stood straighter as he continued, "Maybe we can have lunch tomorrow." His words came out more like a statement
than a question.

"Yeah, maybe," were the only words she could say as Adam reached and pulled her close to him. It was meant to be a friendly hug, but once their bodies touched, heat soared through Adam's body. He couldn't help thinking how good she felt in his arms. She fit perfectly. She felt as if someone had poured gasoline on her already burning fire. She was in his arms, a place she had been dreaming of. Knowing she should pull away, she took a step backward as their eyes locked. She was afraid he could see deep into her soul and knew that she wanted to feel his lips against hers.

Slowly his face moved towards hers. He was gong to

kiss her! "You should stop him," her mind screamed. "It's just a kiss," her heart pleaded. Her heart won.

His mouth was pressing down on hers. He had imagined kissing her, but never in his wildest dreams could he have imagined how sweet she could be. Somewhere deep on her mind, she heard a voice that was not her own. She struggled to hear it again to make sure it was real. There it was again. "Uncle Adam. Brittany," came the words from a sleepy Scotty.

Hastily, Brittany and Adam released each other. They knew this was something that Scotty should not have seen. It would only add confusion. Still relishing in Brittany's kiss and not quite sure what to say, Adam simply answered his nephew. "Yes, Scotty?"

Before Scotty could answer Adam, Brittany interrupted. "Adam, I should go." Se left so quickly that neither he nor Scotty had time to say another word.

"Adam bent down and picked Scotty up. "I'm sorry about this, little buddy. You should never have seen that. Let me try and explain this to you." He carried Scotty over to the couch and sat down with him. "I don't want this to upset you," Adam continued. "Sometimes grownups do things without-thinking. Brittany and I are very close, but we shouldn't have kissed. I'm really sorry if this upsets you in any way." He gave his nephew a hug for reassurance, although he wasn't sure whom he was reassuring, Scotty or himself.

Scotty pulled back and answered, "I'm not upset, Uncle Adam. I wish Brittany didn't leave. I wanted to thank her for today." He looked so innocently at Adam. "I wish Brittany lived with us." Then his face turned solemn "I also wanted to tell you that I had a bad dream about Mommy and Daddy."

Adam noticed the tears in Scotty's eyes and felt crushed

for him. Hatred for his sister and her husband seethed inside him. Swallowing hard, he forced himself not to show Scotty the anger he was feeling. He kissed his nephews' forehead. "I'm sorry you have to go through this kind of stuff, Scotty. I know in here," he said as he touched Scotty's heart, "you love your Mommy and Daddy and miss them very much. You may never understand all that has happened to you. One day you will know that living with me was the best thing for you. I promise. It will take time, but as time passes the hurt won't be as bad as it is right now." He smoothed Scotty's hair back with his fingers. "Do you want to talk more about your dream now?"

Scotty rubbed his eyes with the back of his hands. "I just keep dreaming that they are being mean to me. I keep yelling for you, but you never come. It's so scary."

Adam watched as a tear trickled down Scotty's cheek. "I'm always going to be here for you. I know it must be scary for you in your dream, but it's just that, a dream. In real life I am here for you." He took Scotty's hand and placed it over his own heart. "I love you and will always love you. You will never be mistreated again."

These words satisfied Scotty.   Suddenly he hopped down and made a mad dash for the bathroom. Rambunc-tiously he yelled out, "Can I have a bubble bath now?"

"What was I thinking!" Brittany scolded herself. She had felt so awkward standing there in front of Scotty. She had had to get out of there! As she undressed to shower, she en-gaged in a raging argument with herself. She felt the need to wash Adam's touch and kiss off herself. The cologne he wore still overwhelmed her senses.

The blinking answering machine reminded her that she had missed four of Blake's calls today. She had no idea how she was going to explain why she had not answered her house phone or her cell phone. The familiar feeling of guilt was already beginning to take over again. She should not have spent the day with Adam. She knew she had made a mess of things now.

The water was too hot, and it burned her just as Adam's kisses had. She should have stopped his kisses as quickly as she stopped the scalding steam of water. But she hadn't. Instead, she had stood there like a foolish teenage girl allowing Adam the pleasure of her kisses.

With dinner over and Scotty in bed for the night and the evening gone, Adam was alone with his thoughts. His mind wrestled with his heart about what Brittany was thinking this very minute. Was she missing him or was she hating him right now? He knew deep down he shouldn't have touched her, much less kissed her. It had felt so right, but he knew it was wrong because she was engaged to Blake. Yet he longed for her. He wondered if Blake realized what a wonderful, beautiful woman he had in Brittany.

Brittany awoke hoping to feel better about what had happened between herself and Adam. To her dismay, she felt worse. Last night she had returned Blake's calls, expecting to find comfort in his voice. Their conversation was geared towards his dad instead of her whereabouts for the day. He also told her he had run into her best friend, Lissa. She had made him promise to tell Brittany to call her.

After speaking with Blake, Brittany pulled out her address book and looked up Lissa's number. If anyone in the world could make any sense of this mess, it would be Lissa. She promised herself to call later.

Morning passed slowly for Brittany. She knew she had agreed to lunch with Adam, but she couldn't make herself call him. Yet, she didn't feel right about ignoring him either. She
98

had no idea what she should say to him. She also knew she had been selfish in leaving him to explain things to Scotty. She felt maybe she did owe him the lunch after all.

Instead of forcing herself not to think about Adam, she decided to let her mind wander freely. She needed to understand why she had not stopped Adam from kissing her. She recalled when she had first seen him how taken she had been by his handsome image. She remembered how impressed she had been to find out he was Scotty's uncle and so willing to change his life to care for his nephew.

She went over everything and then she asked herself again how she could kiss another man while engaged to Blake. She had been fighting her feelings from the start and now began to realize she might falling in love with Adam. She had no idea how she would handle this. She still also loved Blake.

Although he felt as if he owed her an apology, Adam did not call Brittany that day. He had hoped she would at least call to cancel lunch, but she hadn't. He came to the conclusion she was upset with him. As she should be. A gentleman never acts the way he had.

Chapter 15

Blake drove slowly by her apartment and saw her bedroom light was still on. That usually meant she was reading a book. He could tell when he had spoke to her on the phone that something was wrong. His thoughts were bitter. *I know her well enough. I bet it has somethig to do with Doctor Wonderful. What I wouldn't do to get her completely away from Adam. I wish there were some way I could make Brittany dislike Adam.* He twisted his lips into a grimace.. He hadn't yet figured out how to make that happen.

"Brittany!" Blake said louder than he probably should have for being in a hospital, but the elevator door was closing, and he didn't want to miss her. When she heard his voice and pushed the button to hold the door open, he hurried to get in fast. "Honey, how are you? I missed you these last few days." Blake dropped his briefcase and hugged her tightly.

Trying to sound as if she had no guilt at all, she responded. "Blake, I've missed you too. How's Robert?"

Sensing the hesitation in her response to his hug, he released her. "We think he's going to be just fine. You know him. Nothing holds him down for long."

This was harder than she thought it was going to be, but she forced herself to continue. "Is Sharon still holding up well? Did you give them my regards?" Nervously, she smoothed an imaginary wrinkle in her blouse.

"Yes and yes," Blake answered. "You know those two.

They'd break their necks trying to do for one another. That's how their love has always been. They both say hello to you."

He watched as she fidgeted with her clothing. "Dinner later?" The elevator door opened on the third floor just as Brittany agreed to dinner. She stepped out and wasn't sure why she glanced over her shoulder at Blake before leaving. Something is definitely up, Blake grumbled to himself. He would make it a point today to run into the good Doctor if it was the last thing he did! He wanted to see if he had a nervous fidget too!

Rounding the corner to the next patient's room, Brittany bumped into Adam. She could tell this was not going to be one of her better days.

"Excuse me," she said as she made her way past him. "I wasn't really watching where I was going."

"Brittany, wait," Adam said. "I'm sorry. I really wanted to call you yesterday and tell you that I was sorry. I knew you were upset with me. I really do apologize for what happened."

Brittany released the door handle to the patient's room. She certainly didn't want the patient to overhear this conversation. "No need to apologize. It was as much my fault as it was yours. I'm the one who is engaged here. No hard feelings."

Adam felt responsible for the chilly tone in her voice. "I won't let that happen again. You have my word. I need you to know that I do respect you, and I do respect the fact that you are engaged. I don't know what came over me."

Adam released a sigh and shook his head. There was no need to lie to her. "Brittany, actually I do know what came over me, but that still doesn't make it right. I admit, I am at-

101

tracted to you. Again, that doesn't make it right."

Those were the last words she wanted or needed to hear come out of Adam's mouth. "No, it doesn't," she said. "I'll talk to you soon. But not here, not now."

She opened the patient's door and walked in. "Hello, Mrs. Bay. How are you feeling today?"

So something had happened between them, Blake had told himself. When the elevator stopped on the fourth floor, he realized he had forgotten to pick up paperwork form the third floor nurse's station. He stepped aside to allow room for a mother with a baby stroller and then pushed the third floor button. Exiting the elevator, he headed towards the nurse's station, but stopped when he heard Adam's voice. It was eavesdropping to stand around the corner and listen to their conversation, but he just couldn't help himself. He needed to know what had happened, and now he did. He renewed his vow to himself to do anything to keep from losing Brittany.

She would never belong to another. With a new hatred for Adam, and a deadly look in his eyes, he picked up his paperwork and headed to the elevator.

When Adam caught a glimpse of Blake as he entered the elevator, he wondered if he should catch up to him and talk with him man to man. Before he could decide on his answer, the intercom announced he had a phone call. He went directly to the nurse's station and answered the call.
"Hello, this is Adam Franklin," he said as he noticed the stares of the nurses.

"Dr. Franklin, this is Jenny Calloway at Saxon Elementary. We need you to come right away. We've had a problem with Wes Fields."

"I'll be right there," he answered anxiously. He directed

102

the nurses to inform the other doctors that he had an emergency and must leave at once. When Adam arrived at Scotty's school, Wes was still there, along with police officers. He was yelling something about people taking his son from him. Immediate concern for Scotty entered Andy's mind. Wondering if Scotty had seen his dad, he ran past the offensive scene and into the school office. Trying to sound calm as he approached the desk where the two ladies stopped typing to look up at him, he declared . "I'm Adam Franklin. Where's Scotty Fields?"

One of the two ladies stood and introduced herself as Jenny Calloway. "I'm so sorry about all of this," she began nervously. "Scotty is fine. This mistake was made because we have a girl from the temp agency here with us today to take over for a worker who is ill. When Mr. Fields came in and wanted to check his son out, she thought nothing of it. She checked his ID,their names matched, and she called Scotty to the office. When Scotty entered the office he started yelling that his dad wasn't supposed to be here. The principal and I both came out of our offices to see what all the commotion was about and were faced with a very drunk and disorderly man. I immediately took Scotty into the office while Mr. Lewis, our principal tried to handle Mr. Fields. When I saw things were getting more out of control, I called the police. Next, I called you."

Jenny could tell that Adam was very agitated by what had taken place. "Again, I'm very sorry," she said.

Adam knew it had been a mistake. Nonetheless, harm could have come to Scotty. Taking a second to regain his compusure, he looked out the window. Then he turned around, sighed and looked at Jenny. "Please tell Scotty that I am here and will see him in a moment? I need to go outside and try to deal with the police and Mr. Fields."

He walked out to where Wes was still ranting to the police about seeing his son. "Hello Officers." Adam extended his hand. "I'm Adam Franklin, Scotty's uncle and legal guardian."

Having greeted the officers, he now turned his attention to Wes. "Why are you doing this to Scotty? This just makes it worse for him. Don't you think he's been hurt enough?"

Wes staggered against the patrol car. "You think you are so high and mighty, don't you, Adam?" he accused, pointing a finger at Adam. "What do you care about my son? You're just using him to get that fancy girl you're falling for. Me and Carol, we want the boy back, one way or another."

One of the officers stepped towards Wes. "Mr. Fields. You can't go against a court order. You no longer have custody and to take the boy will be considered kidnapping. Do you understand that?"

Making his hands into fists, Wes spoke, "I understand Adam and his fancy girlfriend stole my kid from me and my wife. I ain't gonna stop trying to see my kid!"

The officer grabbed Wes's arm. "Consider this your lucky day, Mr. Fields. With Adam's okay, I'm going to allow you to go home and sleep this one off. When you wake up, think about what you're doing to the boy by this kind of behavior. Stop drinking and clean yourself up. Think about what's best for your son."

Wes jerked his arm from the officer's grasp and walked towards the car where his wife, Carol was waiting. Wide eyed, Carol asked," Did ya see him? How'd he look? Does he want to come home with us?"

Wes slammed the car door shut. "Shut up, Carol and just drive! I'm awful thirsty. Do we have anything in this stinking car to drink? Just listening to your long-winded brother
104

makes my mouth bone dry. We ain't never gonna see our boy again if your brother and that fancy girl have anything to say or do about it!" He laid his head back against the seat and closed his eyes. "Just drive?"

Nurse O'Reilly stopped Brittany in the hallway. "Is Dr. Franklin back yet?"

"Back yet?" asked Brittany, her face showing puzzlement? "I didn't know he had gone anywhere."

Oh," Nurse O'Reilly replied. "He had an emergency at his nephew's school."

Brittany didn't waste any time before she raced down the hall to the elevator. She wanted to get to the school as soon as possible and nearly ran right past Blake.

"Brittany," he called out!

She really didn't want to stop and chat with Blake, but she knew she couldn't just ignore him. Slowing her pace, she said a quick hello, hoping to be able to continue toward the elevators.

"Where are you going in such a hurry? I didn't hear a STAT announced." He knew exactly where she was headed, since he had overheard the nurses talking.

Feeling a little on edge, Brittany readjusted her scrub jacket for no apparent reason, and feeling a little own edge, she answsered brusquely, "No, no STATS. I didn't realize I was walking so fast. I guess I was sort of preoccupied with my thoughts."

Realizing she was lying, he struggled to be calm as he asked, "What happened to Adam?" He watched as she tried to hide the concern for Adam showing in her face .

"Adam? What happened to Adam?" She was aware of her voice cracking.

"Huh. You haven't heard." His voice dripped with sarcasm. "It seems the boy's daddy showed up at school. You didn't know?"

Why was he getting such pleasure in seeing her squirm? she asked herself. "No, well, I did hear something about an emergency at school, but when you said Adam, I thought something else had happened. I was on my way to see if Scotty was okay."

Blake crossed his arms over his chest. "I'm sure the boy is fine. I understand that Adam took him from school and is going to spend the rest of the day with him." Walking toward her, he uncrossed his arms and patted her on the back in a mocking gesture. "There, so now you don't have to wonder or worry any longer. He's in good hands." Blake rubbed the bottom of his chin with his open palm. "As a matter of fact, I was going to stop by there on my way home today. Care to join me?"

She had no doubt that Blake suspected something had happened between her and Adam. One of the nurses could have overheard her and Adam's conversation and then reported it to Blake. That's generally how rumors ran their course in this hospital. Brittany looked towards the elevator, wanting to escape this whole scene with Blake right now. "I really shouldn't. I think   maybe Scotty just needs to be alone with Adam for a while.Besides I have to stop off at the grocery store if we are having dinner at my place tonight."

"Now, Brittany, you don't have to pretend with me any more. I know how important that boy is to you. He will be so
106

excited to see you."

How much longer can I keep up this charade? she thought on her way to Adam's house. Blake had acted strangely all day, and when she had once again tried to back out of this trip, he still insisted she come along. So here she was on her way -- good or bad -- to see Adam with Blake following closely in his car.

When Adam opened the door, he was shocked to see Brittany and Blake standing on his porch. "What a nice surprise " was all he could manage to say. He invited them in and called out to Scotty to inform him they were visiting.

Brittany's mind went back to the last time she had stood in this very spot. Although she forced herself to stay, she wanted nothing more than to leave. Blake noticed the thick tension between the two of them and admitted to himself he was getting some enjoyment out of watching the two of them squirm a little.

"Scotty, look at what I brought you," Blake said as he pulled a stuffed animal from behind his back. How clever he had been to stop in the hospital's gift store this afternoon. He would have a better chance of gaining the boy's trust if he brought him presents.

Unaware of his motives, Scotty happily took the stuffed animal from Blake and thanked him. "I'm going to my room now and introduce him to all of his new friends," he exclaimed as he ran down the short hallway.

"Adam, what happened today?" Brittany was determined not to let her anxiety get the best of her. Plus she still had not heard the full story of the school incident. "He seems fine."

Adam guided them to the family room and offered

tea, water or coffee. He left through the side entrance to the kitchen and returned with a tray of drinks. Taking a sip of his iced tea, he began "Well, to answer one of your questions, Scotty's therapist says as long as he talks about what happens while he's at therapy, he doesn't have to talk about it here. She said I should never try to force him to speak about anything he seems reticent to talk about."

Feeling the need to be included in the conversation, Blake interrupted. "So did he see his dad at school?"

Adam told them how the mistake had happened because a specific form had not been placed in Scotty's file. This form would have stated the school could not release Scotty to anyone other than himself. He explained that the temp had not known about the form.

Blake wasn't as interested in this subject as he appeared to be. He hadn't forgotten about the conversation he had overheard. But he still enjoyed watching Brittany try to act as if nothing had happened. He could tell she was very nervous, while Adam was playing it off quite well.

Brittany had heard and seen enough. Now she was ready to go, satisfied that today's event had not seemed to traumatize Scotty. "Blake," she said, " we should really be going. We have taken up enough of Adam's evening. I still need to prepare dinner. Let's go in and say our goodby to Scotty."

Throughout the next day at work, Brittany managed to aboid both Blake and Adam. But her luck was about to run out as she saw Adam walking towards her.

"Hey," he called out to her. "Where have you been hiding all day? I wanted to ask you something."

"Questions", she murmured too quietly for him to hear.

108

She wasn't ready to answer any questions about what had taken place between them. She stopped, placed her hand on her hip and replied, "Go ahead. What's your question?"

Adam sighed heavily. "Hmmmmm, bad mood? I just need to know what time you and Blake will be bringing Scotty home tonight."

Adam's question baffled her. "Bringing him home?" She shook her head. "I didn't know we were taking him out."

Now it was Adam's turn to feel awkward. "Yeah, I ran into Blake earlier and he asked if he could pick up Scotty from school. I already called the school and made the necessary arrangements."

"I haven't seen Blake since dinner last night, nor have I spoken with him." She was trying to figure out what Blake was up to.

Adam scratched his head and looked around to make sure no one could hear him. "You didn't tell him, did you?"

"Of course not, Adam. He's just returned form visiting his father, who had a mild stroke. He's been under a little stress these past few days, so I certainly didn't want to jump right in with both feet and add to it. Plus, he's not going to be exactly happy when he finds out what happened between us. Questions, there will lots of questions."

She stepped inside a vacant room and sat in one of the chairs. Adam followed. "Maybe that's why he wants to spend time with Scotty. Sometimes Blake has odd ways of apologizing to me and making things up to me. He may figure if he spends time with me and someone I care about I'll forget that he was upset with me and things will be normal again."

Adam had to agree that would be a very strange way

to apologize to someone. He hated the sad look on her face. More than that, he hated the fact he could be the reason for her sadness. He knelt down in front of her and looked into her face. "Brittany, I'm very sorry for my part in this. I didn't mean for anything like this to happen. I did fall in love with you, but I sure didn't mean for you to find out like this. Not now. Especially since you're engaged."

She felt tears building in her eyes and wanted to explain to him how she felt. "Oh, Adam, I'm sure by now you know that I have feelings for you, too. I'm so confused by all of this. I can't and won't place all the blame on you. It's my fault too. I know Blake is hurting and now you are hurting. This isn't how it's supposed to be.

Adam reached over and wiped away the tear that was trailing down her cheek. She took his hand in hers and held it to her face.

During the rest of the day, Brittany did not hear from or see Blake. She couldn't understand why he had told Adam they were picking up Scotty. He hadn't spoke to her about this. Now she could only assume he had meant to go without her. She'd go home, try to relax, and figure out this mess she had gotten herself into.

Blake had left a message on her answering machine that he hadn't been able to locate her after work to tell her about picking up Scotty. She knew if he had really wanted to, he could have just called her cell phone. *He hasn't really tried. In his message he doesn't even say where he's taking Scotty. That's another way of making sure I can't join them. But why? Maybe I should call Adam.*

"I thought you would have gone with Blake and Scotty," Adam told her. "He called and said that he couldn't find you after work but that he would leave a message as to where
110

they were going so you could meet up with them."

"He left a message, Adam, but he didn't say where they were going."

"This worries me a little. Why wouldn't he want you to know where they are?" Adam began putting his shoes on.

Brittany was overcome with a sinking feeling, thinking now that he had never intended to take her along. "This doesn't look good," she mumbled to herself as she started to prepare what she would need to go out. She would investigate.

Not hearing her voice, Adam thought perhaps they had been disconnected. "Brittany? Hello!"

Adam's voice jolted her back to reality. "Adam, do you think Scotty would talk to Blake about what he saw the other night?"

"Well, I guess. If he was asked. I did explain to him the other night that we had made a mistake. But I never told him that he couldn't tell anyone." Why?"

She started to cry softly. "I think it was his intention all along to be alone with Scott. This way he could freely question him."

Adam wasn't sure what to be angrier about -- the fact that his nephew was being used to get information or the hurt that Blake was causing Brittany. His voice was clipped as he asked, "What do you want to do about this, Brittany?"

"I'm coming over over to your house to wait for their return, Adam." They sat in silence waiting, knowing there was only a small chance that Blake would refrain from asking the child any questions. They knew that no matter what, they would experience an awkward situation. She would have to explain why she was here with Adam.

Brittany scolded herself for not being honest with Blake about kissing Adam. "What a mess this is."

At the same time, Adam felt he was mainly responsible for this whole turn of events. If only he had shown more self-control. But looking at her, even now, that was hard to do. She was dressed in jeans that hugged her slim hips and a thin tight t-shirt. The exact shape of her perfect breast pressed against the material, seeming to beg for his attention. He wanted to offer her comfort, but knew he couldn't attempt that without going further. He imagined the situation getting totally out of control.

As he suffered pangs of regret, Scotty pushed open the door and entered just before Blake. "Uncle Adam!" he exclaimed with excitement. He then noticed Brittany. "Yay, and Brittany is here too!" His shiny little face made her forget for a moment why she was here, but it was only for a moment. Blake didn't look quite as happy to see her as Scotty did. She couldn't blame him. At this moment, she wasn't ex-actly happy with herself either.

The three of them listened as Scotty told about his eve-ning with Blake. To Brittany and Adam's surprise it sounded like a very fun time. Blake had taken him to play video games and then had gone for ice cream.

Brittany knew she should be going and readied herself to leave when Blake rose up saying he should also be on his way but suggested to Brittany that he would stop by her place and bring dinner from their favorite take-out restaurant diner.

During dinner, Blake asked her, "So, how was your day

112

at the lake? You never did tell me much about it, Brittany."

When Blake scooted his chair back from the dinner table, she nearly choked on the drink of water she was trying to swallow. *Here it goes*, she thought.

"The lake was beautiful and not as crowded as I had expected. And as you can see by my lasting sunburn, the sun was out all day."

"Anyone there you knew?"

"No, I can't say there was," she replied. She didn't want to do this, not now, not ever.

Blake wiped his mouth with his napkin. "Mentioning sunburns, did you see the sunburns on Adam and Scotty? What do you suppose they were doing over the weekend to get so much sun? Any ideas?'

There was no reason to keep this going any longer, she thought. Somehow he had found out about their lake trip, or maybe it was just a good guess. But it was time to come clean.

"Okay, Blake. I didn't tell you Scotty and Adam came to the lake with me. I had called Adam to see if I could bring Scotty with me. When I got there Scotty pleaded to have Adam come along with us. So he joined us. You've had a rough last few days and I didn't want to upset you any more that you already were. I really don't see the big deal. I thought it would be fine."

"Upset?" Now why do you think that would upset me?" Blake scowled as he stood up. "And what do you think by say-ing you thought it would be fine? Wasn't it?"

113

By the way his eyes flashed, Brittany could see Blake's temper. She wanted to put an end to this once and for all. "That's not how I meant it! I just meant that I thought it would be fine for him to join us. Fine with you, Blake, that's what I meant! It seems everything I do these days must be okayed by you first or you get angry."

His face was mottled red with fury. "Angry! I'm not supposed to be angry! What, you didn't think spending the day with Adam would upset me as much as your receiving roses from him? Or have you forgotten about the roses! Of course you haven't. You just thought that I had forgotten. All right? Is there anything else I should know while we're on this fine subject?" He slammed his hand down hard on the table.

She had never seen him this enraged, and she found the scene he was making somewhat frightening. At the same time, she felt he had no reason for being so angry. She retorned by standing up and facing him. "First of all, Blake there is no need for such actions. And for your information I did not know the roses were from Adam until the day we went to the lake. I thought you had sent them. Why would I think Adam would send me flowers?"

She was flustered. Needing something to do, she began clearing the table while he paced the floor, still grumbling and waving his arms about. "Do tell me, Brittany, why is another man sending the woman I'm going to marry, roses?"

She turned to face him. "He said he had sent them to show his appreciation for all I had done for Scotty. Is that so bad? As for your other question, the answer is no. There is nothing else I should tell you!"

He grabbed his car keys from the counter top. "Nothing you should tell me, or nothing I should know about. There's a difference, Brittany! I'm going to go now because I think I should be alone to sort out some things. You just remember, you are engaged to ME!"

As Blake stormed out the door Brittany yelled, "Why didn't you just say the roses weren't from you!" Of course there was no answer. She didn't really want to lose Blake. But then again, she didn't want to lose Adam, either. Brittany sat on her couch alone in the dark for hours after this, with churning thoughts running wild.

Feeling she needed to confide her thoughts with someone, she thought about calling Adam, but then she sat down again. That wouldn't be fair to Blake. Maybe she should talk to her mom? No, she would just worry if she thought Brittany was having problems. Then she thought she had a brilliant idea. She would call Lissa, her old friend. She might be able to help her sort out her thinking. It would be great to connect with her again.

Chapter 16

"Brittany. It's good to hear your voice," Lissa squealed at the surprise of Brittany's call. "How are you? Blake told me he thinks you put in too many hours at the hospital."

Brittany's mood was not as jovial as her friend's and hoped her voice would not reflect her feelings. "I'm doing well. How are YOU?"

From Brittany's tone of voice, Lissa thought her friend was up to a much-needed girl talk, so she plopped herself in the middle of her king- size bed prepared for a long session. "Oh boy, do you ever sound down in the dumps. Though not much worse than Blake did when he was here. He tried to wear a happy face, but I saw right through it. I thought it was because of his dad's illness, but listening to you, I know better now. So, come on, spill the beans. What's going on with the two of you?"

Brittany spent the next thirty minutes filling Lissa in on the whole story, not leaving out a single detail. She was crying now. "So you can see why I'm so confused."

"Brittany," Lissa said sympathetically, "this isn't the first time this has ever happened to someone and I'm sure it won't be the last. Keep in mind that you and Blake have been together forever. He's your first true love. We never want to part with our first loves." Lissa pushed for a moment to reflect on a love or two of her own. "Don't be so hard on yourself. Sometimes people grow up and realize what
116

they thought was the real thing, isn't at all."

They talked for quite some time. They talked out different scenarios and their outcomes. It helped, but Brittany still didn't have a solution as to how she was going to handle the fighting with Blake that was sure to happen before this whole thing was over.

"You know, Brittany, if things get too out of hand, you could always come here. I have a spare room you could stay in. The hospital here could certainly use you. You might want to give that some thought."

Brittany thought she could surely entertain the thought of staying with Lissa. Being back in her hometown didn't sound like such a bad idea. She would definitely miss Blake, and she knew she would miss Scotty and Adam just as much. To think that Scotty had somehow been thrown in the middle of all of this was breaking her heart even more. Running away probably wasn't the best answer, either. But was wanting time to think really considered running away?

As Brittany entered the hospital cafeteria, she instantly regretted her decision not to eat elsewhere. She saw Adam seated to the right of the main entrance. Turning her head slightly, she suddenly caught glimpse of Blake entering the side entrance. When he saw her, he immediately started towards her.

"So, Brittany," he began, "I hope you've been spending some time thinking."

He stood directly in front of her, ready to stop her should she try to walk away from him. She raised her hand in a motion to stop him from coming any closer to her. "Blake, we shouldn't really do this here."

When she stepped to the right, he immediately did the same. When she stepped the left, he also followed. In all the years she had known him, she had never seen this side of him.

"Blake, please excuse me," she said quietly, trying not to let anyone overhear her.

"I just asked a simple question. Why can't you answer it?" He knew his actions were wrong, but he, too, was hurting badly. He couldn't stand the thought of losing her. He just needed to know she was just as worried about losing him.

"I can answer that," she said. "First of all, I can't believe you would stoop so low as to bring a small child into this. How could you do something like that?"

"Oh now, hold on," Blake said, his voice a little louder than it should have been. "I asked you if you had anything else you wanted to tell me, and you said no. But there is something else, isn't there?"

Adam had been watching the scene unfold between Brittany and Blake, feeling there was no need for him to get involved. That is, until he heard the tone in Blake's rising voice. He just couldn't sit at his table and let her take what sounded like the brunt of Blake's anger. He rose and slowly approached the couple.

"Blake " he said, "listen..."

Blake glared at him. "I knew you were trouble from the start. You need to go back to your table. This does not concern you." Blake stood with his chest out and his arms to his sides with his hands balled into fists.

Adam would not allow Blake's stance to intimidate him.

118

"Oh I think it does concern me. And I will not leave until we talk calmly about this." Adam stood just as tall and straight as Blake, not budging an inch.

Brittany was hating herself for what was happening right now. Squeezing herself between the two men, she placed an open palm on each man's chest. "This kind of behavior from the two of you will not get us anywhere. So it will stop as of right now!" She held tightly to the rush of courage she was feeling at this moment. "I will be the one to end all of this hostility between you two."

She could feel the tears stinging her eyes, but she willed them not to fall. "Let's just sit down like civilized adults."

When the three of them were seated, at the square table, Brittany took a deep breath and began to tell Blake everything that had happened on Saturday, the day at the lake. She explained to him again how Adam's invitation to the lake was innocent. She told him about their racing on the beach, playing with Scotty. She told him everything, not leaving out a single detail. Then came the part she had never wanted to tell him because she knew it would hurt him tremendously.

But she knew she had to, and with an expression empty of any emotion, she faced both men as she spoke. She could see from their change of expressions how her description of the kiss affected each of them. It showed on both their faces. Blake's scowl seem to soften and she saw a cocky half smile form. She knew her words had boosted his ego. On the other hand, she saw Adam's shoulder slump and a dullness creep into his eyes. Her words seemed to have crushed his usual demeanor.

Blake was the first of the men to speak. He looked at Adam still smirking. "You should never make a move on another man's woman," he grumbled.

Adam did not allow Blake to intimidate him. Still remaining calm, he declared in a self-confident voice, "I have already apologized to Brittany and I'm apologizing now to you. I had no right..."

Blake cut Adam's apology short. "I don't care about your apology! It means nothing to me, I just wanted to hear the truth from Brittany. And as far as Scotty goes. I didn't involve him. I admit that I did plan the evening so I could question him. But then I couldn't make myself go against my beliefs in using a child in any circumstance. You see. I overheard your conversation at the hospital. I just didn't know how far the two of you had actually taken things. I had to know. When I was out with Scotty, we spotted a couple kissing at the park. He said he had never seen his Mom and Dad do that. He went on to make the comment that he'd only seen his Uncle Adam and Brittany kiss. His innocent statement stung me. Even after he spoke these words, I still never questioned him. You see, I really did have a good time with the boy. Although it started out to be a plan to find out more about you two, it didn't end that way."

Disgust showed on his face just as quickly as the softness had fallen only a moment before. Blake stood up, ran his hand through his hair and spoke directly to Brittany. "I knew you would be worried and be waiting at Adam's when I returned with Scotty. You're not as good at hiding guilt as you think you are." He turned his head to Adam and back to Brittany. "Neither of you are. And Brittany, our engagement, wedding, and our lives together are on hold until you get your head back on straight. I have no intention of giving up on you. I couldn't bear to see you with anyone else. But I won't be made a fool of again!"

Before either Brittany or Adam could comment, Blake

was out the door. Brittany started to go after him. Then she changed her mind. Hadn't she done enough damage?

"Adam," Brittany said, as she stared at the door Blake had just passed through. "I should go. I'm sorry to have put you through this. I can assure you it won't happen again."

"Wait," Adam pleaded. "I'm fine. It's you that I'm worried about. I'm so sorry for all the trouble I caused you." He took her hand in his. "I just want you to be happy."

Brittany promptly pulled her hand out of his grasp. "Goodbye, Adam." And with that, she left, knowing exactly what she must do.

Chapter 17

The news spread quickly around the hospital, like hot syrup. Brittany was gone. She had left both her lovers behind.

Blake could hardly bear the absence of the woman he loved, and he wanted to follow her. He knew her well enough to know that isn't what she would want. She left to have a chance to think things through, and his showing up on her doorstep would only hinder that. He just hoped that she wouldn't have much thought when it came to Adam Franklin. He would do the thinking when it came to the good doctor, and right now his thought was to get rid of him.

The news of Brittany's decision to leave town hurt and shocked Adam. He couldn't believe Brittany would leave without a word to Scotty. He wanted to go to her, but he knew she needed time to herself. He would have to wait it out. Unfortunately, he would be waiting with Blake watching his every move. That was okay because he had no intentions of letting Blake out of his sight either.

Brittany had spent the first couple of days with her parents. Rick and Nancy were pleased to have their daughter home again, if only for a short time. They knew she was under stress and supported her decision to spend time back in her home town. Robert and Sharon Daniels were not quite as understanding. They wondered how Brittany could just up and leave Blake, the man she supposedly loved.

Lissa convinced Brittany to move in with her. Although

it was most likely a temporary arrangement, both were glad to be in each other's lives again. Within two weeks of her move back to her home town, Brittany was in the full swing of things at her new job at Landfair Hospital. She was putting in many hours of work, but she still had time to make a few new friends. She missed Blake badly; nevertheless, she still thought of Scotty and Adam constantly, reminding herself every minute that she was doing the right thing.

"Brittany! Good. You're home!" Lissa squealed when she heard the front door close "I've been dying of curiosity. You have a letter, and it's postmarked Saxon!" Lissa picked up the letter she had placed next to herself on the end table. As Brittany approached, Lissa handed it to her and watched as her friend stared at the envelope a few seconds before opening it. Brittany had immediately noticed the lack of a return address.   Not knowing which man she really hoped it was from, she felt hesitant about opening the envelope.

Lissa observed Brittany slowly peel the envelope open. The envelope's contents existed of only one piece of paper. She saw Brlittany stare blankly at the paper for a few seconds before her face became very pale.

"What is it, Brittany? Who is it from?"

Brittany didn't answer, but she held out the paper to Lissa with shaking hands. Then, with lips trembling and eyes open very wide, she stared at Lissa and shakily replied. "I don't know." She handed the paper to Lissa for her to try and make any sense of it. Lissa took the letter from Brittany's trembling hand and read the four words that had not been hand written, but typed.   HOW'S LIFE BACK HOME?

At first, Lissa didn't understand either. Taking a moment to think, she said, "I get this! This man only wants to know how you are. He didn't identify himself because he wants you to decide who it's from. You know, like which one pops in your head first kind of thing."

"Don't you think that's a bit weird, Lissa? Not to mention just a tad bit creepy." Brittany shook off a chill that produced goosebumps on her arms. "

Lissa smiled. "No, not really. Well. Who did come to mind first? Blake or Adam?"

Brittany frowned and scrunched her mouth to one side. "I'm not sure. I think I was too shocked to think at first. I was expecting an entire letter, not four words typed in bold print."

"Well...okay then. Who do you hope it is from?"

Brittany shook her head from side to side. "I don't know. This is all making me so crazy. I just want time. I know that I love Blake. But it's not fair to him if I have feelings for someone else. I want and need the opportunity to sort this out."

He made the drive from Saxon only to make sure Brittany was still in Landfair. He didn't want to take the chance on her just up and moving again without a word. Sitting across the street from the apartment where she stayed with her friend, he watched the shadows behind the
thin closed curtains. He could clearly see the outline of two people and their movements. She should have received his envelope today and maybe, just maybe, she was reading it at this very moment.

It was a Friday night, and Lissa thought it was time Brittany had some fun. She knew she was still shaken up over the note she had received. Lissa knew exactly how to get her mind off her problems. They would have a blast if she could get Brittany to go along with her idea.

124

"Uh, I don't know, Lissa. I haven't been to a dance club in a very long time," Brittany whined when Lissa suggested they go out dancing.

Hands on her hips, Lissa replied, "Come on, we'll have a great time! We'll get all dressed up and look gorgeous. We'll dance, drink, laugh and tantalize men. Trust me, it will be a blast."Lissa made a pouty face at Brittany.

Brittany rolled her eyes at Lissa. "Yeah, that's what I need. One more man in my life."

Lissa laughed. "I said we'd tantalize them, not fall in love and marry them. Come on, it will be fun. Besides, it will take your mind off things for a while."

Brittany eyed herself in the mirror. She hadn't been dressed like this in ages. She had to admit she felt very sexy in her tight mini skirt, low cut blouse and spiked heels. Out of the shower, Lissa headed for Brittany's room. *Just like old times*, she thought as she caught Brittany primping in the mirror. "Wow! You look sensational!"

Startled, Brittany swung around to face Lissa. "And you look..half naked! I guess some things never change." Brittany laughed. "You still don't mind walking around in scanty sleepwear, huh?"

Lissa laughed and playfully ran her hand down her body. "No reason to cover this up. Someday, someone is really going to appreciate all this."

Brittany had to admit Lissa was just as beautiful as ever. She was still slim, yet curvy. Her breasts, set high and firm, were outlined by thin tan lines from what looked like a very small bikini top. She had the same thin lines that framed her small waist and remarkable backside. *Yep,* Brittany thought,

125

Lissa is one beautiful woman. If I were a man I guess I would want her to parade around half naked all the time Maybe I'm the one that's a bit prudish and old-fashioned. When I'm with Lissa, I, too dress differently.

"You really think this is okay?" Brittany turned to inspect herself again in the mirror.

Tapping her forehead with the palm of her hand, Lissa replied, "Girl, yes! Now I'm off to get ready and hope I look half as good as you."

Brittany forced her eyes to stay focused on her own image in the the mirror instead of Lissa's as she walked out of the room.

The club was crowded and smoky as they entered. It took them a few minutes to find a couple of empty seats. The music was so loud that Lissa had to shout above it. "Hey, what do you want to drink?"

As the waitress brought back their orders of vodka and orange juice, all Brittany could think about was the headache she was most likely to have in the morning. She couldn't remember the last time she had been out drinking. And to think Lissa did this sort of thing all the time.

Brittany was on her second drink as she watched her friend dance with yet another partner. Like the other two, this guy was also good looking. Actually, Brittany noticed, most of the people in the club were good looking. If she were single like Lissa, she would hang out here all the time too.

Lissa danced her way back to their table. Pulling Brittany by the arm, she insisted, "Come on, girl, you can't sit here all night. Dance! Have fun!"

Once on the dance floor with the music blaring, Brittany began to have fun. She let herself go as she herself danced with different partners. Lissa and she even did a routine dance they had made up when they were in high school. They danced in sync with one another, then held hands and danced provocatively. Everyone roared. It was a great time and it would be a very long time before people forgot that Lissa and she had been at the club that night.

Leaving the club, Brittany knew she was more than a little tipsy. She hadn't been smart like Lissa and quit after a couple of drinks at the beginning of the evening. Lissa laughed as she helped her into the car. "Enjoy this feeling, girl, cause you won't feel this good come morning."

Brittany slurred her words. "I know," as she fastened her seat belt. Squinting her eyes, she noticed something underneath the blade of the wiper. She unfastened her seat belt and stumbled out of the car to retrieve it. It was an envelope with BRITTANY written across it. She held on to the envelope tightly while fumbling with the car door handle. Finally she managed to get herself back into her seat.

Lissa sat behind the wheel, watching her friend's actions. "What is it?" she asked.

"I don't know. Probably something from a guy we were dancing with. We can read it on the morning."

The euphoric feeling of the alcohol was beginning to wear off. Closing her eyes, she rested her head against the seat. When she slightly opened her eyes, all she could see was the inside of the car spinning. Mumbling unknown words, she fell into a deep sleep.

The next morning Brittany awoke in her bed wearing only her bra and panties. It took only a second for her to realize she had an excruciating headache. Carefully, she stumbled into the bathroom. As she fumbled through the medicine cabinet, she dropped a compact mirror.

"That's seven years bad luck, you know," Lissa said, walking into the room. "How do you feel? Hung over?" Lissa covered her mouth to muffle her snicker. "You look awful."

"I have a very bad headache. Where in the world do you keep your aspirins or anything that will kill this pain in my head?" Brittany looked at Lissa through half closed eyes and grumbled. "Really? Will you never change?"

"Follow me," Lissa said, Brittany tried to avert her eyes from Lissa's half-nakedness. She had never met anyone who loved being almost in the raw as much as her friend. Had her head not felt as if it was going to pound her to death, she would have actually giggled. Still, no matter how much pain she was in, she couldn't refrain from asking, "Could you please put something else on?"

Brittany stopped and seated herself at the table, listening to Lissa's devious laugh in response.She closed her eyes and rested her head in her hands.

"Here, take these. You'll feel better soon." Lissa opened a bottle of headache medicine.

Brittany reached out her hand to take the pills from Lissa but instead accidentally grabbed the bottle, which overturned slightly, dropping some of the pills.

Lissa laughed and let out a fake groan. "Hmm...mmm. I think you had a little bit too much last night. You'll learn to control how much next time.

Quickly, Brittany retrieved her hand. "Grrrr!" She glared

at Lissa through half opened eyes. "Cover yourself up and give me the freaking pills!"

Laughing even more loudly, Lissa reached for her robe and wrapped it around herself. "I'm going to make you some dry toast. It will settle your stomach. In the meantime, why don't we find out who your secret admirer is."

Peeking through her fingers, Brittany said, "Huh? What secret admirer?"

"Remember, last evening Brittany? The envelope."

Brittany strained to remember last night and vaguely recalled a note under the wiper blade. She took the envelope and opened it, blinking her eyes several times to make them focus on the note she found inside. It read: JUST CHECKING ON YOU. THIS WILL ALL BE OVER SOON!

"What is this supposed to mean?" Brittany cried as a feeling of uneasiness came over her. She tossed the note towards Lissa.

Lissa read the note and then asked, "What will be over soon? Is this one of them backing out, you think?"
Brittany, maybe you should call both of them later. Try to find out which one of them has followed you here."

In need of more sleep, Brittany forced the note to the back of her mind as she made her way back to bed. She fell into a restless sleep where she dreamed of Blake and Adam over and over again. Her dream would take her to a place where she would be in Blake's arms and reach to kiss him, only to find she was kissing Adam, and vice versa. In another instance, she was walking down a path in her wedding gown when she came to a cliff and saw Blake and Adam staring at her. Simultaneously they pushed each other over the edge. She awoke startled, her hair wet with perspiration, her body trembling. She pulled herself together, went to the kitchen and made coffee. She had to be wide awake for what she must do now.

"It's good to hear from you," Blake said when he heard Brittany's voice on the phone. "How are things going? I miss you, you know." He was glad to hear from her, yet he wondered if she had also called Adam. They talked for quite some time. Blake never gave any indication that he had sent her anything via mail or been in Landfair. She, of course did not mention the notes to him. She did admit to herself that she missed him. But she needed answers before she could say those words to him.

She ended the call with Blake thanking her for calling him and telling her he hoped she would call again soon. She then punched in Adam's number on her cell phone.

"Scotty and I are fine," was Adam's response to Brittany's first question after he answered the phone. Most of their conversation revolved around Scotty. Adam informed her that Wes and Carol had been allowed a supervised visit with their son. He told her how Wes had made a comment that he was glad the fancy girlfriend had left town. They talked a few moments longer. Adam gave her no reason to believe he had been the one to send the notes either. She had no idea, nor could she sense, which one of the two were lying.

....

Since talking with Adam and Blake a couple of days ago, Brittany had been racking her brain. She still could not figure out which one was telling the truth. Definitely one had sent her a note and even driven to Landfair to leave a note on her car. She was about to place a call to Blake when the doorbell rang.

"I got it." Lissa yelled as she went to the door! She greeted the local florist who handed a box and said, "These are for a Brittany McNeal"

"Who was at the door?" asked Brittany as she entered the foyer. Her eyes searched the small area for a third person.

"Florist." Lissa murmured, handing her the box she held.Curious to see who had sent them, Brittany took the box. Not finding a card from the sender, she untied the pretty red bow neatly placed around the box. Opening the box,she found six long-stemmed roses bundled in thin gray wrapping paper, Black roses! Stapled to them was a note that read: YOU SHOULDN'T HAVE MESSED WITH MY LIFE! I'LL PUT ROSES LIKE THIS ON YOUR GRAVE BECAUSE OF HIM!

Brittany's face turned pale -- almost stark white while chills ran up her spine. Dropping the box, she felt her body tremble uncontrollably as tears welled up in her eyes. She was scared.

Lissa reached for her friend to catch her because Brittany looked as if she might faint. Holding on to her she asked. "Black roses? What does the card say?"

Afte helping Brittany into a chair, Lissa bent to retrieve the card. Pulling it loose from the leaf, she read it and then turned to Brittany in shock. "Oh my God, Brittany! We have to call the police. This is a threat on your life! It has to be either Blake or Adam. But no matter, this just turned very serious."

Brittany told the entire story to the police officers twho arrived shortly after she placed the call. She started at the point when Scotty had entered the picture and ended where she had left Saxon. She then explained that since she had been in Landfair, she had received two other notes but at first had not been alarmed because she knew they had to be from either Blake or Adam. She did not leave out a single detail.

The officers explained that an investigation would start immediately. They also advised her not to hesitate calling if she should receive anything else or see either Blake or Adam in town. They left her their business cards with cell phone numbers highlighted.

Chapter 18

Blake wanted so badly to call Brittany, but he felt he needed to give her time. Although he missed her, he would wait. As he was debating whether he should give in, he thought "Why not visit my parents? At least I would be in the same town. And, if I'm seen in the same town I will have a legitimate reason for being there." He immediately began to pack for his trip.

Brittany tried to go about her every-day life as usual. But she had become wary and looked over her shoulder constantly. The police still had no answers. She couldn't understand why either Blake or Adam would take things this far. Neither of them had ever shown signs of cruel behavior, but the stalker couldn't be anyone else. She had no enemies -- only these two men who were trying to outdo each other and were making her nervous. What if the one who was doing all of this found out he was being watched. Would that make him angrier?

It was dark now. Again, he sat across the street watching her apartment. It was time, he thought, to send her another present. He laughed silently to himself. He'd show her! "She just can't wreck a man's life that easily without having to pay a price." He was speaking loudly to himself inside the car.

"Blake, what took you so long to get here? You're forty five minutes late. I was getting worried." Sharon Daniels was the type of person who always expected everyone to be on time. She had been pacing the last three quarters of a hour waiting for her son to arrive.

Blake kissed his mother's forehead. "Yes, Mom, I know and I'm sorry, but I had a flat tire. Then I remembered I had removed my spare for extra storage one day. I called a tow truck, gave the driver directions to where I was and then found my phone had died. Sorry for making you worry. But I'm here now." He took his mother by the hand and guided her towards the kitchen where he knew she would have something delicious waiting for him.

"Brittany! Brittany," Lissa yelled as she entered the apartment! "Are you here?"

Brittany came running from her bedroom. "What is it?" she asked?" Then she spotted the envelope in Lissa's hand. Fear seized her body, and she began to tremble involuntarily. "Not another one," she said in a husky whisper. "Why is this happening to me?"

Lissa stepped in closer to hug her. "I don't know, honey, but we need to find out." Releasing her, she placed the envelope in her hands. "You have to open it. We need to see what it says."

Brittany looked down at the envelope as if she were holding something evil. Her hands trembling, she slowly began to open it and pulled out a single white folded paper obviously torn from a spiral notebook. Unfolding the paper, she read IT'S BEST YOU FORGET ABOUT HIM! YOUR LIFE DEPENDS ON IT! Her voice came out in sobs as she flung the paper away from her.

Lissa grasped Brittany's arms. "Brittany, look at me. For starters, we are going to call the police, just like we were told to do. They will handle this." Lissa reached for the phone.
134

One of the same detectives, James Kelly, came to their apartment some thirty minutes later. He was glad to,be delivering shat he thought was good news. "We may have caught our man, Miss McNeal," he announced in a proud voice.

Brittany sighed. "You mean it's over? Which one is it?" She wanted to know the answer. She wanted to know who was capable of playing such dangerous mind games. She wrung her hands and squeezed them so tightly that she felt pain.

Detective Kelly spoke. "We followed one of the men into town last night."

Brittany reached for Lissa's hand as she held her breath. She knew she would need the physical support when she heard the answer.

"At first, when we followed him into town, our man lost him on the highway. However, he did manage to get his tag number, so we could find him again. I have Detective Gary Addison questioning Blake Daniels even as we speak."

Brittany went numb. Her shock made her feel faint at first. Then her fear began to turn to anger, and she regained her strength and managed to remain standing.

"Blake!" she exclaimed. "I should have known. He has been acting so strangely lately. Do I get to see him? Do I get to ask him why he did this to me?"

The detective had already begun to do his job, confident he had the right man. When he went to Sharon Daniels' home, he introduced himself and asked for Blake. Curious as to why a detective would be seeking her son, but sure it was probably a friend or something regarding his work or patients, Mrs. Daniels called out to him. "Blake, someone here to see you. Could you come downstairs, please?" She invited the detective to have a seat in the living room.

Blake was not so happy. Someone had apparently seen him even though he thought he could get by for at least a few days without attention. Yet someone was here. He quickly came down the stairs and was shocked to see a man seated on the couch. He was even more disturbed
when he saw the badge hooked to the man's belt. It clearly stated he was a detective. Blake smoothed down his newly grown mustache. "Detective, what can I do for you?"

"I would like to know where you were last night." Detective Addison pulled out an electronic tablet from his briefcase. "What time did you arrive here? Have you left your this house since you arrived?"

"Wait a minute," Blake roared in anger. "What's this all about? I left Saxon yesterday, late afternoon. On my way here I got a flat tire on the highway and I didn't have a spare. A tow-truck driver... a Billy something or other helped me. We took the tire, filled it with air, put it back on my car and I was on my way again by eight o'clock." Blake leaned against the wall and raked his hands through his hair in frustration.

Seeing the detective's lack of trust in her son, Sharon became angry. "It's true. He arrived here at exactly eight forty- five." She balled up her fists as she spoke earnestly. "He called me from Saxon as he was leaving. He should have been here at eight, but the flat tire made him late. Now would you mind telling me why you are treating my son like a criminal?"

Sharon Daniels was not about to let someone come into her home and treat her son as if he were a street thug! Detective or not!
136

Detective Addison knew he could not reveal too much about why he was questioning Blake. He shifted his attention to Blake, neglecting to answer the mother. "So, you agree with your mother that you arrived here at eight forty-five?" He typed something into the black tablet as he waited for Blake's answer.

Blake nodded his head. "Yes, and I haven't gone anywhere since I arrived.

Detective Addison finished typing and placed his tablet back into the case. "Of course, I'll have to check out your story and a couple of other things. I'll get back to you. In the meantime, don't leave town without letting our police department know." He turned to go and then pivoted back suddenly, as if he had forgotten something. "By the way, do you know a Brittany McNeal?"

Now the detective really had his attention. Blake felt his heart accelerate. "Of course, I do. Has something happened to her? We may not be seeing eye to eye on everything right now, but we are engaged."

Blake stepped closer to his mother. "I came here yesterday to visit my parents because not so long ago my father had become ill. I ..uh... didn't even want Brittany to know I was in town. That's why I haven't left the house since I arrived. Please tell me she's OK."

Detective Addison took note of the beads of sweat on Blake's forehead. That seemed odd to him. It was not warm in the room. He kept a poker face, though, as he left. "Then there shouldn't be any problems with your story. As for Ms. McNeaL, she's fine."

Sharon and Blake watched as the detective drove away. They stood arm in arm, both quietly letting their thoughts simmer at the oddity of circumstances.

Since Detective Kelly had not followed up since he had left her apartment the day before, Brittany was becoming apprehensive. She did feel very lucky, though, to have Lissa by her side as a great support. She still couldn't understand why Blake wouldn't give her the same support. Didn't he know that his attitude was chasing her away instead of helping them bond?

She thought of calling Adam, just to hear his kind voice. But just in case Blake had an unquestionable explanation for being in town, she decided to take Lissa's advice not to call Adam.

Deep in thought, Brittany barely heard the doorbell. Going to the door, she peered out the small window pane before opening it and felt reassured when she saw it was Detective Kelly. "Helllo, Detective. Is it over? Did Blake say why he had taken such drastic measures to scare me?"
She started to ask another question, but the detective interrupted her.

"Brittany." Detective Kelly gestured towards the living room. "May I come in?"

Brittany stepped aside and led him inside the room. Eager to hear his answers, she had to keep reminding herself of her manners. "May I get you a glass of water or tea?" she asked, already anticipating his answer.

After Deective Kelly declined anything to drink, he cleared his voice ad began. "Brittany, it doesn't appear that Blake is responsible for any of this. The story he gave us checked out. He did have a flat tire and since his arrival has not left his parents' home."

Her heart sank. This is not what she had expected to hear. Not that she wanted it to be Blake -- she had just wanted it to be over. "What now," she asked? "Does this mean it was Adam?"

"Well," Detective Kelly cleared his throat. "I've checked with my men, and they reported back that he hasn't done anything out of the ordinary. He spends a lot of time with his nephew. It seems he is having some trouble of his own with a Wes Fields. I understand Fields is the boy's father."

She crossed her arms over her chest, hugging herself protectively. "Wes Fields is Scotty's father. He and his wife have an alcohol problem."

She got up and began to pace, changing the topic. "What are we going to do now about these threats? Which one is covering his tracks very well?"

Detective Kelly released a sigh. He wanted to get this solved for Brittany. He could see the fear and worry in her eyes.

"I know this is unpleasant for you. Please bear with us on this. It could be that one of them has hired someone to scare you. We are getting the go-ahead from the judge today to place a tap on each of their phones. I'm sorry, but it's really all I can do for you.

The detective finally left Brittany standing there feeling hopeless. Lissa walked up to her and put her arms around her to try to comfort her. "I can't believe that one of them has thought this thing through so thoroughly." Lissa's voice was full of concern for her friend.

Brittany wiped a tear from her eye. "I know. That's the scary part. I just don't know what to do. I just cant believe this is happening." Finally, she let go with sobs jerking her body.

When Lissa hugged her, she was thankful to be here with her.

Adam was frustrated. He wished Brittany were back in Saxon. Scotty missed and needed her. She had her own special way of cheering the boy, and Adam felt he needed hat, especially now that Wes was giving them such a hard time by showing up everywhere they went. The last days he strangely had left them alone: however. the strain was wearing on them both.

He worried even more since he learned that Blake had gone off to Landfair to visit with his family. How convenient, he thought. Thinking of Blake so near Brittany made Adam's temperature rise.

Chapter 19

"I have no idea how I let you talk me into this again! I'm not drinking tonight like I did last time!" Brittany straightened her mini skirt as she headed towards the dance floor for the fourth time in the last hour.

"You need this!" Lissa's voice rose above the roar of the loud music. It's good to get your mind off things for a while. Tonight, let's just dance!"

Lissa began dancing and pulled the nearest dancer in between them. Brittany gave a loud whisper meant only for Lissa's ears. "Lissa, suppose he didn't want to dance?"

As Lissa gyrated,when she went near Brittany she answered. "Why should he mind? He's only dancing with the two best looking girls in the club!" She laughed as she wiggled her hips seductively."

As they were getting back into the car at the end of the evening, Lissa asked, "Did you have a good time tonight, Brittany?"

"Even better than last," she answered. You're too much. Plus I won't be waking up with a terrible hangover in the morning." Brittany opened the mirror on the visor to do a quick check of her makeup. It didn't matter that they were heading home. She flipped the visor up just in time to see a car headed straight for them.

"Lissa, watch out " she screamed!

A car with its bright headlights blinding them was heading straight for them. Lissa tightened her grip on the steering wheel as she tried to swerve out of the path of the car. Her quick reaction saved their lives.

When the danger was past, Lissa stopped the car and bowed her head over the steering wheel. She expelled the breath whe had been holding. Then she looked up at a white-faced Brittany who eyes had grown enormously and whose teeth were chattering from fear.

They got out of the car for a moment to regain their balance. "Thankfully we were smart enough not to drink and drive, unlike that poor soul who must be heading for an accident. I wish I had been able to see the license number.

Still shaking, Brittany asked, "Do you think that's all it was? A drunk driver?"

Lissa shrugged her shoulders and gave Brittany a skeptical look. "Sure I do."

Brittany shook her head. She was not convinced. "Well, it could be someone trying to get at me."

"Now come on, Brittany, you have to keep your head about this. Notes and black roses are one thing. Trying to hit someone with a car is entirely different. That would be attempted murder. Don't start being paranoic. "

After a brief rest, Lissa began to drive again down the same highway. As before, Brittany saw the bright lights in her side mirror. "Oh yeah. Well that car is coming back! I can't make out the car because of the lights. What are we going to do, Lissa?"

142

This time Lissa noticed the car appeared to be speeding as it came closer. She had a strong hold on the steering wheel and focused on her driving, speaking softly through clenched teeth. "We're gong to stay calm. We'll let whoever it is follow us right to the police department. It's only about six blocks from here."

Filled with fear now, Lissa drove cautiously with the other car following as close as possible to their back bumper. The too-bright lights of the car continued to make it difficult for Lissa to see the road. Brittany asked, "Why don't you speed up so that we can lose them?"

"I don't think it's safe to do that, Brittany. The driver will only accelerate and put us in even more danger. Instead, I'm driving directly and slowly to the police department." In a few minutes, she made a quick right hand turn into the street where the police department was located. Brittany was glad to see the car behind them continue speeding straight away.

"See?" Lissa declared. "They figured out where we were taking them." They made a quick getaway.

Once inside, Brittany and Lissa asked to see or speak to Detective Kelly. They were surely a sight to behold in their mini skirts and high heels. The officer on duty did a double-take when he saw the two girls enter the department. He had to admit they were very good looking in their little skirts that showed off their long legs. At first, though, he did a double-take, thinking they were "ladies of the evening" in trouble.

When he heard their voices, and noticed the startled look on their faces, he became concerned and came from behind the desk to greet them. "We need to speak to Detective Kelly right away. Please," Brittany bellowed! "He told us to contact him immediately if we had any more problems. Well, we definitely have more problems."

143

"Please, as soon as we can, we need to see him. Is he here?" Lissa looked around the empty room.

The officer on duty looked form one girl to the other. "Okay girls. Try to calm down some and explain what has happened. First. Let's start with your names. Have a seat. You're safe here."

When they were seated, he listened intently as the girls gave a full account of what had just occurred. Twenty minutes later, Detective Kelly walked into the station looking as if he was still half asleep. It was only one thirty in the morning.

The girls repeated the evening's activities. "The person could have killed us!" Brittany sobbed.

"Okay, ladies. I'm going to make a couple of calls. Stay right here and try to relax." Then he turned to the other policeman. "Officer, could you please get these two ladies some water?"

After a while, Detective Kelly returned with a puzzled expression. "So...it looked as if both men have been occupied with their jobs all evening. We checked their phone lines, too, and neither has been calling from the private cell phones, either."

He took a seat facing the girls and looked at them seriously. "The only thing I can think of is that maybe the person used the hospital phone or his mother's phone."

As they looked at him, dismayed, he stood up again and walked a little circle before turning to them and putting up a hand. " It's also possible that this is a completely separate incident from the previous ones." Giving them a wry smile, and then a little grimace, he asked, "Did you girls dance at the club with a guy that might have wanted more
144

than a dance? Perhaps somebody half-lit got a little upset or possessive and wanted to intimidate you and then, when the person saw the police station he became more intimidated, lost his nerve and left?"

He ran his hands through his hair. "I know this counds crazy, but it IS possible. Lots of crazies out there. Girls should be wary today, especially at night and try not to go unescorted."

The girls felt this was a slight reprimand and, while they could not agree, they had no reason to ask for any more consideration.

Two days after the episode, they, too, began to think the whole scenario had just been a fluke, and they returned to work. Just as a precaution, however, Detective Kelly asked for an unmarked police car to be posted near their apartment. The police department had taken it more seriously than the girls had thought.

The patrol car helped the girls feel more secure, and that evening they both relaxed at home. Brittany settled herself in bed to read the the newest romance novel from her favorite author. She had purchased it earlier at the grocery store, and now her eyes eagerly skimmed across the pages as she heard her favorite country music in the background and the splash of Lissa relaxing in a hot tub of lilac-scented water.

Both girls felt at ease, not realizing their nemesis was in the vicinity. "Just let it get a little darker," he mumbled to himself. "This letter will surely get to her. After she reads it, she won't want to see him again." He gave a low, devious laugh and muttered, "Maybe I won't have to drive here again until I make my final move."

The dispatcher at the police station was working on a crossword puzzle, enjoying a rather slow night. Suddenly, his quiet time was interrupted by a shrill call, "Requesting back up on 34th and Spruce. Looks like our man is about to pay a visit." Immediately the dispatcher notified officers in the area to respond. He remembered also his instructions to call Detective Kelly if any trouble occurred at this address.

Detective Kelly made it to the station just as the officers were bringing in the suspect they had picked up outside Brittany's apartment. His strong voice called out orders. "Take him to interrogation room three. Don't call Brittany until we find out what his story is. Has he said anything yet?"

Officer Grady shook his head. "Not a word. Won't even give us his name."

Inside the interrogation room, he sat motionless and silent, letting his eyes wander around the gray cement calls until they reached the extra large miror on the wall. He knew it wasn't really a mirror. On the other side would be police officers staring at him, trying to figure him out. He grinned with sarcasm, shrugged, and turned his head, staying in this position until Detective kelly entered the room and pulled up a seat directly in front of him.

"You were seen sneaking around from a parked car across the street from the apartment occupied by Brittany Mc-Neal. Want to tell me what you were doing there? Or do you want to start by giving me your name so that I can have it on record? I know you have already been read your rights, so we can proceed."

The man shifted in his seat and stubbornly remained quiet. His eyes wandered from the detective to the mirror.

Detective Kelly had no patience for this kind of behav-

146

ior. He wanted some answers, and he wanted them now. "So which whacked-out boyfriend are you?"

The question seemed to have struck a nerve. The man blinked, but his eyes remained fixed on the mirror. "I'm no whacked-out boyfriend," he stated through clenched teeth. " I just wanted to make sure she stayed away from him. That's all. You know how it is." Leaning back in his chair so that the two legs were off the floor, the man turned and glared arrogantly at Detective Kelly.

Kelly stood up, walked around the table, looked down at the prisoner and shoved his chair forward. The front legs landed hard against the floor, causing the man's chest to hit the table as the detective growled, "No, I don't know how it is. Why don't you tell me!"

The man had heard of things like this happening before -- cops letting cops beat up on people. This caused him to consider that perhaps he should give an answer before the interrogation became more violent. Slowly, he began to explain why he had been stalking Brittany and trying to scare her.

An hour later, Detective Kelly exited the interrogation room and called Brittany. He didn't give her any information over the phone except that they had caught the man who had been harassing her and that she needed to come to the station right away.

Brittany was uneasy as she entered the station, glad Lissa had asked to come with her. She clung to her friend not only for moral support but for physical support as well. When she spotted Detective Kelly, she headed towards him. "Detective Kelly, is he under arrest?" she asked in a sqeak that revealed her anxiety. Her body trembled as she asked the next question without waiting for an answer to the first. "Which one is it? You didn't say when you phoned."

Detective kelley didn't answer. He merely said, "Follow me," as he walked towards the interrogation rooms. Then he added, more gently, "You really need to see this for yourself."

Brittany entered the interrogation room after Detective Kelly. She stopped short when she saw the man sitting at the table. She was very confused. She pointed to the man. "What is he doing here? What does HE have to do with all of this?" She tapped her foot in nervous anticipation of the answer.

Lissa stood next to Brittany.   She looked from the detective to the man and then to Brittany. She was even more perplexed. "Who is he?"

Detective Kelly spoke before Brittany could answer. "This is the man who sent Brittany the black roses and the notes and also ran you two off the road before following you. He was scared the night you drove to the police station and kept going instead of stopping. But then he became brave again and began lurking around your apartment, ready to torment you again."

Lissa looked at Brittany and shook her head in bewilderment. "So who is he?"

Detective Kelly also asked, "Brittany, do you know this man?"

Brittany walked over to the man seated at the table. Her brow wrinkled.   "We'll of course I know who he is! And I want to interrogate him myself, if you wouldn't mind."

Keeping a safe distance, she lowered herself to look directly in his face. "Why did you do this to me? Why? I did nothing to you." She could feel all of her pent-up fear turning into anger."

The man looked at Brittany.   With glazed eyes he looked directly at her.   "You took my little boy away from me."

"Wes Fields, I did no such thing," she yelled as she slammed her hand on the table. "You and your wife Carol abused him! The system took him from you, and it was for his own good! The actions you have exhibited now make your case even worse. "

Chapter 20

One week later, Brittany arrived back in Saxon. She had already arranged a return to her old job. It felt good to be home again and was extra happy that Lissa had decided to give Saxon a try.

While away from both the men interested in her, she had had much time to think. Her scare in Landfair had forced her to think about Blake and Adam and what was happening in their lives. She understood whom she loved now and would always love. *Love is different from a sexual attraction. Love is constancy and has a lasting quality. When one loves, she must attempt to understand her partner and not bait him to make him jealous. She should listen to his pain and always be open and honest.*

Blake had become insanely jealous when her attention had been diverted to someone other than himself. At first, that had been Scotty, but it wasn't Scotty he had been worried about really. It was Adam. Her love for Scotty had transferred itself also to the uncle since Scotty seemed to need the stability of a couple. Adam, who had never wanted children before, had become an instant father. Having been attracted to her before, he now had looked upon her as the perfect woman to complete the trio and help him with Scotty. He thought because Scotty needed her so much, he had to have her in their lives. She knew Adam wasn't really in love with her. He had seen her once from a distance, and when he saw her again, his nephew already loved her. He instantly thought it was something that was meant to be.

She confided in Lissa. "Adam and I were never meant to be. I have loved Blake for a long time and know that I always will."

As she looked at Lissa, she suddenly had a brilliant idea, but she would not express it openly. She would plan to help out two good friends, but she had to do it sneakily. First, she would call Blake and talk to him. Then she would call Adam and ask them both to meet her in the park near their home by the lake.

On Saturday morning, she and Lissa waited on the bench throwing bread crumbs to the ducks. Brittany turned her head as she heard her name called lovingly. Without hesitation, she ran to Blake and filled his arms with her body. He kissed her long and hard until she remembered their audience and placed her palms on his chest to pull herself away. Looking up at Blake, she whispered, "Just a moment."

He smiled and nodded in the direction from which she had come. Confusion masked her face as she turned to see Lissa and Adam already talking. Her expression changed instantly to a conspiratory smile as with twinkling eyes she looked up at Blake and threw him a kiss

She wouldn't have to be sneaky after all. Lissa pulled Adam by the hand lightheartedly and walked by Brittany and Blake. She whispered something in Adam's ear and ran back to Brittany. She took Brittany aside where Blake could not hear and said mischievously, "I think he's going to love my aftershower attire when you and Blake baby-sit Scotty. " Lissa then ran to catch up to Adam.

Epilogue

The hospital grapevine was in its glory the day of the great wedding reception. The stories of the romantic encounters, as well as the adventures and misadventures of the two couples had been hashed and re-hashed for days, providing much needed entertainment and discussion.

Now, the happy looks on the beautiful and handsome faces of the two perfect couples and their relatives enhanced the golden glow of the sunshine in the park by the lake. Under a kiosk, the two couples -- Dr. Adam Fanklin and his bride Lissa, and Mr. Blake Daniels and his bride Brittany -- exchanged vows at the same time. The vibrations of the sincere expressions of love spoken against a background of soft classical music caused more than one ooh! and aaah! and teary eyes in the assembly.

One of the unusual sights was that of the tiniest and sweetest little flower girls (relatives of one of the parties) and the two young seven year old boys who accompanied them -- all dressed in white. One of the young boys, Scotty, was best man for both couples. Scotty had been adopted by Dr. Adam Franklin and Lissa just the week before after a quick civil wedding ceremony to ensure adoption before the formal wedding.

The ceremony ended on a note that will be long remembered. Immediately after the two couples exchanged vows and kissed, Scotty flew into their midst for a group hug and then turned toward the attendees to announce joyfully, "Yay, everybody! I now have not only a mommy and a daddy but I have another uncle Blake and auntie Brittany to love me. I am the luckiest boy alive."

Who says dreams do not come true?

CPSIA information can be obtained at www.ICGtesting.com
Printed in the USA
BVOW02s2246181115

427721BV00001BA/18/P